VAGABONDESS

A GUIDE TO SOLO FEMALE TRAVEL

Editor: Pavita Singh
Book Design: Zvonimir Bulaja, Booknook.biz
Cover Design: May Phan
Cover Photograph: Casparo Brown
Bio Photograph: Graeme Essen

Featuring work previously published at Elephant Journal, Rebelle
Society, Salon, Thrive Global, and Matador Network.

ISBN
Print: 978-1-7348753-0-0
ePUB: 978-1-7348753-1-7
MOBI: 978-1-7348753-2-4

www.vagabondessthebook.com

VAGABONDESS

A GUIDE TO SOLO FEMALE TRAVEL

TOBY ISRAEL

To your inner vagabondess:
I see you.

"When a great ship is in harbor and moored, it is safe, there can be no doubt. But that is not what great ships are built for."

— Clarissa Pinkola Estes

Contents

Introduction

Vagabond (n)

1

: a person who wanders from place to place without a fixed home : one leading a vagabond life

: moving from place to place without a fixed home : WANDERING

2

A : of, relating to, or characteristic of a wanderer

B : leading an unsettled, irresponsible, or disreputable life

Where it all began...

I used to long for adventure. Sensitive, romantic, fifteen- -year-old me pined for the thrill she knew from books and films. Pirates, nomads, and wayfarers populated my dreams. Already I was searching for something elusive. Not a place. Not a person. A feeling.

And feelings are hard to pin down on a map. Sometimes, you have to spend a whole lifetime wandering in their pursuit. A feeling doesn't have a mailing address. A feeling doesn't come at the end of a "5 Simple Steps" blog post. There is no big red X marking the spot. There's no clear mountain path to its abode.

This feeling has an unmistakable smell: woodfire smoke. A marketplace at noon. Saltwater. Damp earth. Chai. Skin. Old leather. Dusty journals. Sex. It has a sound: leaves crunching underfoot. The hum of a motor. Waves crashing on an empty shore. Human wolves howling at the moon. Tambourines. It has a taste: cinnamon and clove. Blood. Fresh air at 5,000 meters. Cold river water. And it has a color: blue like the sky. Blue like the sea. Blue like veins running beneath the skin's surface, pulsing with life. Blue like twilight—at the edge of everything.

What *was* this feeling, then, in practical terms? Freedom? Close. Weightlessness? More grounded. Romance? Loosely interpreted, maybe? Wanderition (the consummation of wanderlust)? Getting warmer.

If I could give the feeling a name, perhaps I would not have needed to spend so many years seeking it. Yet it escapes every box, category, or linguistic cage in which we try to trap it. The more words I use to try to catch its essence, the farther it seems to recede into the edges of my awareness. It is, simply, *the* feeling.

If you have ever quit your life, sold all your belongings, and bought a one-way ticket to anywhere-but-here, you know *the* feeling. If you are considering doing just that, you know intimately the feeling-shaped wish in your soul. If you know me, you know what the feeling looks like when it takes over a human being and directs her life for a time.

Spoiler alert: you won't find this feeling "out there." It is a state of being, not a destination. Therefore, this book is not a map, but an existential guide to a vagabondish lifestyle and perspective. If you want to hold this feeling in your hands, you will have to dig for it yourself. There is no other way, no shortcut, no online course, no magic recipe. As a vagabondess who has made a life-long study of this feeling, I humbly offer you a few tools that may aid you on your own journey of discovery—and stories to help you on your way.

July 2017—Boston (my hometown)

Question: How do we find our calling?
Answer: We don't.

Question: Okay, but, something more helpful?
Answer: We don't "find" our calling; we call out, and follow any voice that answers until our intuition tells us we can stop calling now. Some of us never do stop.

Question: Anything less esoteric?
Answer: Fine. Seek joy. Seek more questions than answers. Seek jobs, friends, lovers, homes in which or with whom you feel utterly yourself. Better yet, seek experiences that challenge you to become even more yourself—that is, to grow.

And if you should find more growth in movement, do not stop moving. And if you should find more meaning in stillness, stay still. And if at the end you still should wonder if you ever did find your calling, look back over the one inimitable path behind you, and ask your footsteps what you have learned. Hint: The right questions lead not to answers, but to doors. We don't find our calling, we walk it.

A path always makes so much more sense in retrospect. Looking back over the twenty-eight years that brought me to this moment in my life, it seems clear to me that it could not have been any other way.

I had the exceptional good fortune to be born into a family of travelers. I grew up in Boston, Massachusetts, but family vacations brought me to India, China, Italy, England, and many other places before I was out of adolescence. These vacations sparked my curiosity about that *something*, which I felt fairly certain was *out there*, and which I would spend most of my twenties seeking.

I first lived abroad in Paris in 2009-2010 as an eighteen-year-old gap year student. I studied little, explored much, and began to develop a broader understanding of Self there in a big city with plenty of space to get lost... and found. At age twenty, as an Anthropology undergraduate student at Vermont's Middlebury College, I spent four months traveling and studying Tibetan language and culture in Nepal, then took eight months off to wear out a few pairs of shoes. Here, truly, I began to walk my path as a vagabondess. I wove my way along the "banana pancake" backpacker's route through Southeast Asia, then stuck my proverbial neck and my literal thumb out on the road, hitchhiking over 6,000 kilometers through Europe. Why? I've never managed to explain it better than I did in an article I published in *Salon* about the experience:

"I love adventures. Over the course of my year-long journey, they became my raison d'être. I had always wanted to be fearless, and now I had begun to actively seek out and defeat the things that scared me. I got into motorcycle accidents in India. I accepted invitations to strangers' homes in Nepal. I started eating meat again so I could try anything. I hopped buses on an impulse and boats on a whim. I ate street food throughout Asia. I became a "yes woman." I tried to shake free of the platitude that, as a young woman, I must always travel with fear and caution.

By the time I reached Europe in April of 2013, seven months into my trip, the initial euphoria of my solo journey had begun to fade. I crossed the Balkans by bus and train and realized that the simple act of travel had ceased to be an adventure. Trains, which I had loved with a romantic nostalgia bordering on the irrational, had become banal, and that saddened me. I sought to rekindle my adventure.

… As I continued on, my pack became lighter. I gave away clothing to friends, left behind shoes, used up my shampoo and didn't buy more. *I* became lighter. I stopped updating my blog. What could I write about that was not *this*? The physical act of travel, of movement, once more consumed me.

I could, in response to expressions of disbelief and disapproval, argue the statistics: that I was safer on the road in Germany than at a frat party at my college, that my odds of being harmed were so low that I might as well take risks and enjoy them, that I was more likely to get run over by a car, anyways. I could argue that I carried pepper spray, waited at gas stations, and took rides selectively, but those are false securities, and regardless, I made my choice on principle. My decision to hitchhike, and then to continue hitchhiking, sprang not from reck-lessness or a cynical conviction in the futility of caution, but from optimism."

(I still hitchhike, once in a while. It still packs a power-ful punch of travel-induced euphoria. I still believe in the goodness of humanity, too. I will delve further into my personal philosophy of risk-taking in Chapter 1.)

In 2014, I set off on a year-long journey through Spain, Kenya, and Zanzibar. In late 2015, I traveled to Cape Town, South Africa, where I spent most of the next year. In June of 2016, I walked the *Camino de Santiago* in Spain, adding another mode of transport to my list of favorites: my feet. For the most part, I lived out of a six-ty-five-liter trekking backpack and designed my lifestyle to suit my wandering.

In 2017, I moved to Costa Rica to pursue a master's degree in Peace, Media, and Conflict Studies at the UN-mandated University for Peace. Out of necessity and passion, I had developed a location-independent career as a writer, editor, and marketing consultant. Now I decided to dive into the theory behind my work. *How does media work contribute to peace? How are media creators also peace-makers? What does it mean for stories to be medicine?* In a sense, this book is an exploration of those exact questions.

I am still in Costa Rica now as I write this, in late 2019. After finishing my master's program, I decided to focus on designing transformational experiences and retreats, bringing a different lens to travel, transforma-tion, and empowerment. Staying in one place for a while has allowed me to redirect my energy toward initiatives aligned with the vagabondess spirit, such as writing this book and supporting other women to live and travel with confidence. But we'll talk about staying later; there's a lot to be said first about leaving.

In 2018, I completed my Level 1 training as an Empowerment Self-Defense instructor. I now regularly teach workshops and retreats that integrate self-defense training with yoga, wellness, and connection to nature. Now I provide women with practical tools for keeping safe, however they choose to move through the world—rather than simply advocating for taking risks and facing fear. For me, these two principles work in tandem: illogical fearlessness and self-defense-informed confidence.

I have a closet full of metaphorical hats, including facilitator, editor, consultant, dreamer, artist, dancer, organizer, and entrepreneur. However, my "writer hat" has been there the longest of all, ever since I filled my kindergarten journal with fantastical stories and misspelled animals. Two years ago, while flying into Guatemala City from San Jose, the idea for this book popped into my head, a gift from the sunset-hued clouds surrounding my plane. It has been following me ever since.

Now, finally, after carrying *Vagabondess* in my head for so long, I feel it is long past time to set it down on paper.

Welcome to the journey.

Don't Tell Me What to Do

I found my way to this lifestyle through trial and error. I didn't have mentors or guides, only an unwavering certainty that there was another way to exist in the world, and that I was going to find it. This book is for the travellers (current and future), the feminists, the adventurers, the seekers, and the curious. It is the guide I never had, and the advice I probably wouldn't have heeded anyway. In these pages, I offer the insights I gleaned from moving through the world as a vagabondess. It is my intention to provide you, dear readers, with the encouragement we all crave to pursue our dreams, as well as some practical suggestions for getting there.

This is the book I didn't have when I began traveling solo over ten years ago. If it had existed, however, I probably wouldn't have read it. I was seventeen years old, moving to Paris for a gap year before college, and I didn't like being told what to do. I still don't.

I consider stubbornness to be one of my most endearing personality traits, although I doubt many people in my life will agree with me. Nonetheless, my insistence on finding my own way has brought me enough blessings that I'm not inclined to let it go. This tenacity, of course, has also gotten me lost in a few dozen cities. It has led to financial insecurity many times throughout the years. It has landed me in a sweaty mess in hostels and Airbnbs the world over, obstinately walking seven kilometers rather than taking a taxi from the bus or train station. All the same, I wouldn't trade it for the world.

February 2013, India

I am reminded of my arrival to Kolkata at one o'clock in the morning, after a forty-eight-hour train ride from Goa. I had booked no hostel, arranged no transport, asked for no advice from friends with experience traveling in the region. I had read one article about backpacking in India and jotted down the name of a street known for its cheap guest houses. I hopped in a cab, gave the driver the name, and hopped off onto a deserted street.

It had not occurred to me that every single hostel in this city might lock its doors at midnight. I spent a while banging on gates and hollering into empty courtyards with increasing desperation. Finally, a group of South Korean missionaries who were still awake took pity on me and opened the door to their hostel, and a girl my age offered to share her room with this strange vagabondess who had appeared out of the night-time shadows. The next morning, I met two other women who had arrived on the same train but spent the night wandering the streets of Kolkata. They had not been as lucky.

I can't say I learned my lesson. Although nowadays I do try to book ahead if arriving at a new place after midnight. I did reaffirm my faith that humans will (most of the time) help other humans when given the chance—or with sufficient wheedling.

I may be independent to a fault, but I could not have achieved my dreams of being a vagabondess any other way.

It should come as no surprise, then, that I don't like guidebooks. I don't like self-help-style "you must do this to be happy" rhetoric. I really don't like dogmatic, authoritative injunctions of any kind telling me how to live my life. And if my intuition about you, dear reader, is at all accurate, neither do you. So, don't take anything written here as an imperative. I will be the last person to tell you what you "should" or "must" do. You'll figure out your own path; I have no doubt about it. Consider this an interpretive roadmap. My roadmap, drawn with the advantage of hindsight and the lessons from over ten years of experience in being a solo female traveler. I hope it may be of benefit to you.

A Note on Reading this Book

To that end, do not feel obliged to read this book in any particular order. You may read it front to back, or back to front. You may skip the poetry and fiction in between chapters for now, and save those for later. You may ignore them entirely. You may jump around to the chapters or sections that call out to you first. A map doesn't have a beginning or end, not really. And so, neither does *Vagabondess.*

I have given a structure to this book that makes sense to me; that doesn't mean it is the best or only structure. Every mind is exceptional, and I don't pretend to know yours. I encourage you to begin choosing your own adventure right now, dear vagabondess. Read this book however you see fit. I'll try my very best not to tell you what to do as you continue on your journey. Remember: this is not a guidebook, it is a map. Wander at your whimsy.

Feminisms

> "We teach girls to shrink themselves, to make themselves smaller. We say to girls: 'You can have ambition but not too much. You should aim to be successful but not too successful. Otherwise you will threaten the man.' [...]
>
> Feminist: a person who believes in the social, political, and economic equality of the sexes."
> —Chimamanda Ngozi Adichie

Before I dive further into my story, I want to linger for a moment on the subject of feminism. Or feminisms, rather. As mentioned, this book is intended for the travelers and the feminists—ideally both at the same time. I cannot separate my experience or philosophy from this ideology. I believe in equal human rights. I believe in accessibility and inclusion. I believe in cross-cultural learning and respect. I am proud to call myself a feminist, and it is my intention to write this book from a feminist perspective. To me, that entails:

1. **Advocating for the equal rights of all people.**
   In terms of travel, that means both accounting for the many potential factors limiting one's capacity to embrace a vagabondish lifestyle, and bringing awareness to the complex impact of global tourism on local communities and cultures.

11

2. Challenging patriarchal norms of gender, sexuality, age, and ability.

My path as a feminist has a lot to do with encouraging women in particular to break down socially conditioned barriers of fear, doubt, shame, and insecurity. However, this book is intended for anyone who wishes to travel solo and/or challenge the narrow path society has offered them.

3. Offering choices without insisting on the superiority of any one choice in particular.

There is no right path, only your path. It is always my intention to open my readers' eyes to more possibilities than they may have seen before. At the end of the day, however, "my" way is no more "right" than anyone else's. I offer options, not obligations.

In the interest of writing a *feminist* guide to solo travel, I feel it is crucial to address my own manifold privileges. I freely acknowledge every privilege granted to me by my U.S. passport (more valuable than gold), my light skin (opens as many doors as my passport), my age and appearance (hard to measure the advantages of youth and conventional attractiveness, but they are there), and my education (private high school, liberal arts college, and now master's degree from a UN-mandated institution), and my family (I have never worried about supporting anyone other than myself, and I have a safety net in the form of loving, financially stable parents). I do not hide my privilege, nor do I apologize for it. I have received more than my fair share of blessings and opportunities in a relatively short amount of time. I consider it my responsibility to honor the life given to me by living every damn minute of it.

However, to be a feminist means to recognize the varied life experiences of other groups of people. I acknowledge that my experiences as a solo female traveler will be vastly different from those of a woman of color, a woman with a different passport, or an older adult. We each face our own unique array of challenges or advantages. As a woman traveling solo, I have experienced plenty of obstacles and adversities, which I will address in these pages. As a white woman, however, I also find that policemen are friendly and eager to assist me all over the world. As a U.S. citizen, I have an embassy just about anywhere I go that will help me in the case of an emergency. As a professional woman earning U.S. dollars, I hold an uncomfortable position of financial power vis-a-vis many of the communities where I choose to live and work. As a young and outgoing woman, I can easily fit myself into new social circles in unfamiliar places, quickly turning strangers into family. As an able-bodied woman, I typically take my fitness for granted, collecting physically demanding hobbies like my grandfather collected stamps. Nonetheless, these privileges are not superpowers. Underneath it all is a real superpower: human connection. Call me naive, but I believe our humanity is stronger than all the words we have created to divide it.

Finally, being a feminist and an ally also means staying open to feedback and critique. I welcome suggestions on how I can bring deeper awareness, advocacy, and feminist perspectives to my future work. In this book I am doing a lot of talking. I'd like to balance that with a strong dose of listening on the other end of this process. I invite you to reach out to me with your comments, questions, and challenges.

Not a feminist? Let's talk about that another time, shall we?

Why Vagabondess?

July 2016

I'm riding from Sweden to Finland on a ferry named Grace, pondering over aimless wandering. I'll come back to that. Grace is probably ten stories high. She has a club room and a casino, cafes and restaurants, cocktail bars and a dog toilet. She is more floating apartment building than ship, but she floats as she is meant to and she will bring me from Stockholm, Sweden to Turku, Finland in just over eleven hours. For fifteen pounds, that was a slow travel bargain I couldn't pass up.

I'm the foggy kind of tired after a weekend of midsommar celebrations, camping adventures, and repeated sunrise-instigated wakeup calls at 4:30am. The weather sympathizes. Thick clouds crowd the sky and cast the archipelago in monochromatic grayscale. A drizzle comes and goes; the "sun deck" is slick and empty. I sip sour-tasting ferry coffee, which does nothing to clear my head but successfully destabilizes my hands, and watch the procession of tiny islands. Some have just enough space for a single house, while others boast dense stretches of pine forests. I daydream up a contraption that could hitch and unhitch from the passing ferries and allow me to island-hop. (I realize they've already invented one better… it's called a motorboat.)

I'm thinking about wandering. Aimless wandering. In fact, I've been thinking about aimless wandering since it came up in discussion in a wilderness skills training earlier in the month. Actually, I've been thinking about aimless wandering for much longer than that, since one of my first forays into vagabonding in early 2014. It's just that I briefly forgot to think about it until that discussion reminded me.

Already in 2016, my wandering isn't as aimless as it used to be. With so much work to do and so many friends to visit, I plan my travels more often than not. "You're in London in July? Great, I'll come to London in July." "I have one week free after Portugal… perfect, I'll see you in Barcelona." "I need wifi for work this week, I'll just stay in the city."

But there is value in wandering aimlessly. So much value. I still believe that. What is aimlessness? It is space, and it is time. Space to move without restraint or reservation, and time to observe without hurry. Space to expand, in body and spirit, and time to be utterly still. Space for silence. Time for reflection. Space for reflection. Time for silence.

Aimlessness isn't purposelessness. Not to me. Aimlessness isn't meaningless. Quite the contrary. Aimlessness isn't absence from life, it is full-bodied presence in it. To wander aimlessly is to move through the world without the conceit that we actually know what is coming next. That is, to move through the world with grace. (Told you we'd come back to it.)

So here I am, sitting on a ferry named Grace, thinking about aimless wandering. And I'm thinking that maybe aimless wandering isn't a choice, but a description of how we are, all of us, moving through life. Whether we like it or not. Whether we acknowledge it or not.

We don't know what's coming next, but we can go to it with purpose. We can go to it dancing.

There is space to expand, and there is time to be still. Why not embrace it?

———

Why "Vagabondess?" The short answer: because "wanderess" was already taken, and "gypsy" has turned out to be unpardonably off-color. What's more, "wanderers" and all their derivatives—wanderlust, wanderess, wanderlusting—have a bad rap. Trite, overused, lacking in meaning, unserious. Wanderlust is a time of life kind of thing, frivolous, a passing whimsy. Vagabonding is different. It is for life.

A vagabondess has earth and salt to balance her air. Her lifestyle is not a romantic, Instagram-filter utopia, but rather gritty and smeared with sweat. A vagabondess is not a symbol of an ideal of a life. She is alive.

A vagabondess knows "the feeling" with a rare degree of intimacy, and she is willing to share her stories about it. She weaves magic into the everyday and touches the profound with her toes as she wanders—aimlessly, purposefully—through her inner landscape and the outer wilderness of the modern world. She unites nostalgia for a freer past and hope for a liberated future by living squarely in the present tense. For solo female travelers, the vagabondess is an attainable objective, not a holy grail. She is within easy reach, if only we look in the right place: inside.

Why "Vagabondess?" Because no other word fits! I hope soon you will understand why.

———

What do I mean, the vagabondess is inside us? Is that some kind of new-age spiritual metaphorical whimsy? No! Well, maybe it is metaphorical, but the idea is really quite simple. The vagabondess is an archetype, like the mother, the hag, the maiden, and the goddess. She crops up in our folklore and collective imagination, though not nearly as often as I would like to see her there. She represents freedom and radical self-sufficiency. She embodies the qualities of curiosity, optimism, fearlessness, and wildness. Like all archetypes, the vagabondess exists within each and every one of us. To explore the path of the vagabondess is to give space in our lives for these qualities to grow and flourish.

In 2013, I began to write a short mantra everywhere I went: "Be happy. Be free. Vagabond." It emerged organically at some point in my writing, and it dug its claws right into the heart of my travels. I wrote it on hostel walls, bathroom stalls, and sandy beaches. It still sits at the top of my webpage.

I don't think I would have explained it as such then, but I was playing with the archetype of the vagabondess, trying her on for size. As it turns out, she was an excellent fit.

This book is an invitation to the vagabondess inside you to come out to play. I hope you will feel inspired to get to know her.

"Maybe happiness is this: not feeling like you should be elsewhere, doing something else, being someone else."—Eric Weiner

ADVICE FOR TRAVELERS-TO-BE

Don't listen to them. The naysayers, fearmongers, and debbie downers. Don't listen when they tell you it's too dangerous, too difficult, too different.

Don't listen to them… and don't listen to me!

Go and see for yourself. Trust your intuition. It will lead you to purpose and direction. Trust your path. Trust your process.

Discover that everyone is wrong—including you!

Embrace uncertainty, discomfort, and fear. Embrace the not-knowing while relentlessly seeking to know.

Get to know the world. Sit at its feet as it teaches you your Self. Fall in love. Get high on possibility. Become an addict of pure potential.

Be optimistic. People and places have so much more good in them than meets the eye.

Don't listen, don't listen, don't listen—to them.

Bring your ear to rest on your chest, and listen: the whole point is to live.

I. Just Go

Risks, Rewards, & Growing Wings

"Go out in the woods, go out. If you don't go out in the woods nothing will ever happen and your life will never begin."—Clarissa Pinkola Estés

So, YOU WANT TO BE a vagabond/nomad/wanderer/your-word-of-choice-here? Be prepared for a lot of push-back: "Are you crazy? What if something happens to you? Aren't you scared? But is it safe for a woman to travel alone? Won't you get lonely? Homesick? Aren't you worried about the food? The animals? The crime? How will you make money? Where will you stay? Is this really the right time? What are you running away from?"

These questions are probably well-intentioned, but fatal to vagabondish ambition. They seed self-doubt and propagate social myths designed to keep us in one place. There is nothing wrong with staying in one place, of course, if that is what you want to do. However, if the world is singing your song and you yearn to answer it, don't let other people's doubts hold you back.

Are you crazy?

You'll have to be a little bit crazy to ignore conventional wisdom and choose the purportedly more hazardous trail. Embrace that. On ancient maps, cartographers drew dragons to represent all the gaps in their knowledge of the world—the unknown. Today, our maps are painfully precise, and yet, we all have our own dragon-shaped spaces to discover. A fully sane person stays clear of dragons, is cautious with fire, and questions the sanity of others who speak of mythical beasts as if they were sitting right there in the room. A slightly crazy vagabondess seeks out dragons, plays with fire, and jumbles the "real" and the "imaginary" with glee. You'll have to be a little bit crazy to run away from comfort and into the unknown. Whether your dragon is on the other side of the world or one town over is unimportant. It could even be curled up sleeping in a corner of your inner landscape.

Every generation has had its seekers, explorers, adventurers, and vagabonds. Because they are not deterred by superficial problems, such as "Dragons aren't real" and "There are no unknowns left on the maps," they are able to seek and see what others overlook. They have been the believers and inventors, the storytellers and seers. And just because the empty spaces of the maps have all been filled in doesn't mean there are no frontiers left to cross. When I leap into a dynamic acroyoga move that terrifies me, I cross another personal frontier. When I sing in front of an audience, or even a few friends, I cross a frontier of my own ingrained beliefs about what is and is not possible for me. When you do anything that feels uncomfortable, try anything new, or confront anything that makes you afraid, you are brushing flanks with dragons.

When it comes to vagabonding on the physical plane, the key is to move toward our questions. "Aren't you scared?" Step into that. "What if you get lonely?" Explore that emptiness. I am a big advocate for the "learning zone"—that liminal space where the comfortable and familiar end and discovery begins. My learning zone and your learning zone may look drastically different. For some, trying a new cuisine while on vacation is deep into the learning zone. For others, it takes climbing Everest to break out of comfort. Regardless, there is life force there beyond the familiar. A vagabondess seeks aliveness, even if—especially if—that means going through fear to find it.

"The cave you fear to enter holds the treasure you seek."—Joseph Campbell

But is it safe for a woman to travel alone?

November 2016, Chefchaouen, Morocco

One morning during my stay in Chefchaouen, I woke up, ate breakfast on the roof of my hotel, looked at the mountain in front of me, and said, "I want to climb that." So I did... almost. The first twenty minutes of my mission took me on an easy cobblestoned jaunt out of town. The path went as far as a mosque on a hill with panoramic views of the surrounding mountains and the town of Chefchaouen, already far behind and below. After that, I continued on goat paths, overlooking a prominently marked and much easier onward trail, and scampered on. At one point, I encountered an old woman walking in the other direction with her herd of goats. Her head and body thickly wrapped in shawls, she peered out at me with curiosity and stopped to chat. She asked me where I was going (I inferred), and I pointed up the mountain.

She thought I was crazy, but only for going alone.

Are women crazy for traveling alone? Let's break this one down. I'll dive deeper into safety and self-defense in Chapter 8; however, I am also inclined to argue that this is the wrong question entirely. A better question may be, "Why are women conditioned to believe the danger is out there, when in reality it's right here at home?" Globally, the greatest threat to women comes from their own family, friends, and partners. UN Women estimates that, "of 87,000 women who were intentionally killed in 2017 globally, more than half (50,000—58 per cent) were killed by intimate partners or family members." Ninety-two percent of violence against women worldwide is committed by someone known to the woman. Now, this tells me that while "stranger danger" isn't a myth, neither is it our primary threat. We women face greater dangers at home than we do "out there." Yet, who would suggest that we stop dating, marrying, or trusting our families?

As women, we face risks traveling solo. This is absolutely true. However, we also face immense risks simply existing in a world that, to this day, does not protect our basic rights to life and safety. The "solo female travel is just too dangerous" tack is a red herring for me. It assumes we would be perfectly safe if we would just stay home and follow the rules: Dress modestly. Don't go out alone. Don't drink too much. Lock your doors. Don't talk to strangers. This is simply untrue. It also assumes that most people have ill intentions. This is also untrue. Most people are good, kind, and sincere. Traveling solo is a declaration of faith: *I believe in humanity.* We can carry that optimism in our backpacks to distant corners of the globe; we can cultivate that optimism at home. Danger is location-independent. So is trust.

To that end, I have developed my own **theory of risk** through my years of solo travel. It goes like this: All of us choose our risks, all the time. Driving in a car is a risk. (Road traffic crashes rank as the ninth leading cause of death and account for 2.2% of all deaths globally.) Taking selfies is a risk. Approximately 100 people die every year from selfie-related accidents. Smoking cigarettes or drinking alcohol is a huge risk with proven adverse effects on health and longevity. Trusting romantic partners not to harm us is a risk, as explained above.

And yet, most of us choose to engage in many of these and other risky behaviors on a regular basis. It's necessary. It's convenient. The immediate gratification outweighs the possible consequences. Simply put, this *life* thing is risky business. Every individual decides where they want to gamble with statistics, and where they want to play it safe. For me, there was never any question that traveling solo was a risk I was going to have to take. The possible rewards were irresistible. I do not want to live in a world where I cannot trust my fellow human beings. I do not want to surrender my optimism. These twin values—trust and optimism—are largely responsible for the joy and connection I experience in my day-to-day life. And so, I embrace the risks inherent in this mindset. For me, it is the only way I know to be a vagabondess—and to be human.

I invite you, dear vagabondess, to choose your own risks. Your choices will likely look quite different from mine; the important thing is the choosing—making conscious the implicit weighing of risk and consequence that is happening all the time. The key is to choose the risks that bring us into aliveness.

> "Any world is a valid world if it's alive. The thing to do is to bring life to it, and the only way to do that is to find in your own case where the life is and become alive yourself."—Joseph Campbell

What are you running away from?

Ah, yes, this might be my favorite question of all. The simple answer is, don't worry, it's impossible to run away from our issues. Every sadness, heartache, loss, fear, and insecurity I had trailed me down the road of my nomadic life, following my sandy footprints like unwanted travel companions, until I actually took the time to heal, grow, or transform. I have never tried to run away from anything; to the contrary, I am painfully aware that we carry our issues with us until we turn to face them. Sometimes we even have to face them two, three, or a hundred times.

They do not ever simply vanish into an Instagram-ready snapshot captioned, "Let that shit go." It's not that easy.

Vagabonding never solved a single problem in my life. Not a crumbling relationship. Not a fear of heights. Not a longing for security. Indeed, "running away" is an empty promise. Walking off into the sunset, guitar slung across your back, Sufjan Stevens illogically emanating from the empty fields—sorry, it doesn't happen like that.

While running *away* may be impossible, I argue that you should run *anyway*. As far and as hard as you can. With purpose. With laughter. With mad, passionate glee. Wandering isn't a cure, but I believe it is a path. If that path calls to you, sowing iridescent oceans and unfamiliar cobble-stoned streets in your dreams, then honor the call. Wandering won't fix you, but then again, neither will anything else.

Sometimes, we have to come back, go home, stay still to "find ourselves." But maybe, just maybe, sometimes we're waiting to be found at the end of a bungee cord, the top of a mountain, the last hour of an 800-kilometer trail. Wouldn't it be a shame not to go and see?

"… the point is not necessarily that we move to these places but, rather, that we allow these places to move us. I believe, now more than ever, in the transformative promise of geography. Change your location and you just may change yourself. It's not that distant lands contain some special "energy" or that their inhabitants possess secret knowledge (though they may) but rather something more fundamental: by relocating ourselves, reorienting ourselves, we shake loose the shackles of expectation. Adrift in a different place we give ourselves permission to be different people."—Eric Weiner

Is this really the right time?

The best answer to that question is this Kurt Vonnegut quote, which has in many ways defined my journey as a vagabondess:

"We have to be continually jumping off cliffs and developing our wings on the way down."

If I waited until it was the perfect time, I would never do anything! Case in point: writing this book. It's not about being ready, it's about doing it anyway and trusting that we will be able to figure it out as we go along. The "right time" to set off toward a horizon of new possibilities is the moment that you actually go. It's that simple.

Sometimes, we are lucky enough to start building that trust in ourselves young, learning early that we can in fact figure it all out in mid-air. I have the clearest memory of being around four years old and asking my father for help tying my shoes. I was sitting on the bottom step of our unfinished basement, trying to remember something about a rabbit and a hole. And there was my father, who already had all the knowledge I needed about shoelaces and rabbits; he could help me. But instead he said, "You can tie your shoes yourself."

And I did. And I have been successfully tying my own shoelaces for two-and-a-half decades now. Maybe that memory is real. Maybe my mind constructed it out of dozens of memories like it. My parents pushed me to "tie my own shoes" throughout my childhood in countless ways, large and small. It's one of the gifts for which I'm most grateful. I learned very early on that I could face my own dragons, be they rocky mountain paths or snaking shoelaces, and that imaginary wings could carry real weight.

Other times, we have to learn the art of growing wings later in life. Many of us are taught to be dependent on others to meet all of our needs, from the most basic to the most complex. (Of course, asking for help is a good thing, and a necessary part of life. Absolutely. Still, most of us do not want to live in a state of constant dependency.) We often do not learn the art of self-sufficiency until circumstances force us to rely on our own cunning. Regardless of where we are in our process of self-trust, jumping, and growing wings, there are a few key elements to keep in mind:

1. **Balance.** No one is an island all the time. For every cliff we jump off alone, there may well be another to whom we say, "not today," and a third for which we seek a companion to hold our hand on the way down. Balance.

2. **Support.** While my parents were teaching me to tie my own shoes, they were also giving me love and support. I am blessed to know that my family and friends are out there, ready to cheer me on when I fly, or pick me up if I take any knocks on the way down. Family, friends, community—a support sys-

tem, even if we never call on it, makes it so much easier to jump.

3. **Will.** You could argue that personality or background determine our ability to grow wings, and I would disagree with you. While stubbornness is my dominant personality trait, and I don't like following directions, I have met so many others far more resourceful than I, of every possible personality type and background. I don't believe it is personality or circumstance; it's will. Tautological though it may sound, to figure it out for yourself, you have to *want* to figure it out for yourself.

October 2017, Costa Rica

Can this kill me? I've never asked this question so often before, but the diversity of small and threatening wildlife that appears in my jungle house is really unprecedented. Freaky, unnaturally quick spiders on my wall. A black swirly millipede. The spider ants that took up residence in my sink and stove. I check my shoes before putting them on. I catch and release bugs, whose names I'll likely never know, on a daily basis. When I think or write about living in tune with nature, this is the part I always conveniently omit. I don't like these critters—especially when they fly up my nose or bite my ankles—but I do coexist with them. (Maybe that's a good analogy for tolerance; you don't have to like someone to accept their existence.)

And then, these bugs are the part I conveniently forget when I think about how much I love living alone. No one is going to deal with the dead lizard, dead mouse, black widow spider eggs, or the creepy spider-creature if I don't. But that's a good thing, I think.

Traveling alone is a lot like living alone in the woods. No one is going to fix things for you; you have to just figure it out as you go along. Of course, if things get really out of hand, you can always phone a friend. When it comes down to it, to grow wings, you have to grow wings. Will it be easy? That's the wrong question. It's possible, and that's really all we need to know.

Now, let's get to the nuts and bolts of flying. "How will you make money? What will you pack? How will you choose where to go?" These questions bring us to Chapter 2.

UNCERTAINTY (2018)

Uncertainty. How many times must I meet you before I remember your stubborn face?

In work, in travel, in body, in love—nothing is truly stable, not at the core. That is the only certainty.

I have learned this lesson so many times, it rolls off my tongue like a prophecy when I speak to friends and vagabonds-to-be about my lifestyle. Yet, I find I must repeatedly teach myself my own lessons, too.

We're all just human.

We seek, endlessly, for a secure future, a safe home, a lasting relationship, a full stomach, a rich coffer. To do otherwise would render us saints or bodhisattvas. To do otherwise would mean we were no longer human.

The best we can do, then—maybe—is to remind ourselves regularly that our search for certainty is futile… and then to go on searching anyway.

The best we can do, maybe, is to see the humor in it all.

To observe our fallible human hearts and laugh at them— and love them.

Sometimes, I obsess over the practical decisions—where to live, what job or project to pursue, which shoes to pack. I know it is futile to expend so much energy obsessing over something that will change in a day or a year or a season. I know. Each time I jump on the same cycle of thought, I remind myself of this. I stop. And then the next day I start all over again.

It's okay. I'm human.

I note without blame or frustration the patterns in my own life—the relationships where I've grasped at tomorrow, cities where I've hastily sought a room to call home, homes where I've ignored the "here" to plan my escape to "there." I observe all this with a glint of happy laughter.

What a blessing to have arms strong enough to grasp and a heart strong enough to learn, over and over again, to relinquish control.

This journey is really an aimless walk in the woods, but we forget that.

II. Getting Started

All the Practical Things

June 2016, Camino de Santiago

Toward the end of my month-long walk across Spain in 2016, about sixty kilometers before reaching the famous pilgrimage site, Santiago de Compostela, I meet a Hungarian man who causes me to reflect on the idea of the "modern-day renunciate." He walks with two dogs attached to his belt by heavy rope, a huge walking stick clearly decorated and carved by hand, and a fading and unravelling straw Amstel hat. He carries fishing gear, sleeps in a tent with his dogs, and is running out of money. He lost his passport one night in a flood, gave away his watch. His eyes never quite focused on mine, he briefly shares his story:

He had been a farmer. The bank took his farm and everything he owned. So, he left with his dog and started walking. He reached Santiago, then turned around and started walking in the other direction. He concludes, "So probably I will spend my life walking. Just me, the dogs. I think it is good."

I can empathize. If I lost everything like that, I would probably lose any stock I had in property, money, things. I would probably start walking and settle into a state of non-owning, non-needing, non-grasping too. On the Camino, you run into a few of these modern-day renunciates. They're not out for a month-long holiday, or even a six-month sabbatical. They've dropped—or lost—everything, and they're walking, not for a pilgrimage, not for a temporary detox, but for life. I admire them, just as I admire anyone with such a degree of single-minded passion that it borders on psychosis.

More than anything, I'm fascinated by what appears to be a global trend—as the "real world" becomes harder and harder to stomach—of starting to walk (or travel, or meditate) and never stopping. Society has always had its renunciates. They live outside the bounds of normality—normal time, normal family, normal work, normal life—and follow another way. I suppose the only difference is that our modern world doesn't know as well what to do with them. It demands passports. It requires that we identify our place, our role, our function.

Nonetheless, I suspect there will always be renunciates— those who choose not to participate in the world offered to them. It's not a problem; rather, it is for the rest of us to accept and allow their presence there on the narrow paths between the borders of society.

I AM NOT A MODERN-DAY RENUNCIATE. At least not at this stage of my life. On the spectrum of materialism, I tend toward minimalism. My personal philosophy favors non-attachment. Yet, I value my passport. I like beautiful things. I appreciate the food, comfort, art, and experiences I can buy with the fiction that is money. Despite years of lessons on the road, I still try to make plans. I am perhaps irremediably pragmatic.

Most humans are, like me, far from the path of the renunciate. We tend to obsess over the practical questions; thus, most vagabondesses-to-be will want at least some practical answers to the questions: How on earth do you make money? How do you possibly pack for so long in one backpack? How do you know where to go? How do you take care of your health? This book is meant to be much more than a practical guide. I don't want to dwell too long on questions about money, packing, trip-planning, and healthcare, because plenty of those books already exist. However, I realize that uncertainty around basic logistical issues can be a major limiting factor for aspiring solo travelers, so I'll try to touch on the questions I get asked most often.

Making (and Saving) Money on the Road

I vividly remember the relief I felt when I landed my first steady remote job after setting out on the road. Coming on board as an *elephant journal* editor transformed my financial situation from the constant hustle and feast-or-famine mentality of freelancing to a modest abundance of meeting my basic expenses each month. The feeling of weight lifting was palpable. My shoulders relaxed, I stopped running calculations in my head after every meal, I bought unnecessary treats at farmers markets, and went out for coffee just because.

I also vividly remember the anxiety of letting go of that job and the renewed relief with each private client who came my way in the months that followed. I don't know what it's like to have a steady nine-to-five job, but I can tell you that being an entrepreneur, freelancer, self-employed unicorn, or independent contractor is a hustle. That's okay. There is excitement and inspiration in that for many of us. (See Chapter 1.) At times, it is exciting and energizing to juggle a dozen projects, part-time jobs, events, creative endeavors, and private clients. At times, it is exhausting; constant uncertainty and an operating baseline of moderate chaos can wear you down. As of yet, however, I have not felt a desire to trade it for anything else.

But I'm getting ahead of myself. Let's rewind for a moment, since digital nomadism (on the one hand) and renouncing all material possessions and citizenship (on the other) are far from being a vagabondess' only options. For my first forays into long-term travel, I saved up money ahead of time, then budgeted ferociously to make it last as long as possible. It was a good approach for me as I started out, and I think it is a good option for many fledgling vagabondessess. With about $5,000 saved, I traveled for around eight months in 2012-2013. With around $8,000 saved, I traveled together with my partner for nearly a year from 2014-2015. It is possible to do it even cheaper. I often meet backpackers living from day to day, dollar to dollar, trusting that their next meal or next bed will appear and they won't have to use the last twenty dollars in their bank account. I admire these people but have never quite surrendered to that level of financial insecurity. While remote work and sources of steady income can relieve the stress of stringent budgeting, it is undeniably wonderful to travel without thinking about work or needing to carry a laptop. Saving up ahead of a long solo journey is probably the most straightforward place to start for anyone who doesn't have remote work or limitless savings. A few simple choices tend to help:

- **Cut the extras.** Beer, weed, new clothes, meals out, meat, clubs—none of these expenses are actually necessary for survival. Paring down our lifestyle at home can significantly speed up the saving process.
- **Sell it all.** Serious about traveling for a long time? Sell everything you can't take with you. A car alone could easily finance a few plane tickets, if not a whole year of vagabonding. Marie Kondo your life; that is, give away anything that doesn't bring you joy, and find storage solutions only for your most beloved treasures. Everything else is replaceable.
- **Start a Travel Fund.** Mine was an envelope in the closet. I hear there are also more sophisticated options these days with banking apps and other fun technology. Whatever you're earning, take out what you need for basic expenses like rent and groceries, then put the rest into your travel fund.

Myth: You need a lot of money to travel for a long time. As mentioned above, a few thousand dollars lasted me a year, and I know many travelers far thriftier than I. That's a lot of money, but not inaccessible for many earning U.S. or European wages. Depending on your needs, you may want to save more or less, but the "trust fund traveler" is a myth we spread to discourage everyone else from pursuing their dreams of nomadic adventure. (Sure, you will meet people out there traveling who are lucky enough to have years of travel funded for them. But you'll meet many, many more people who just had regular jobs and regular financial burdens, yet decided to go for it, save up, sell their car, or take a risk and hop on a boat with twenty dollars left in the bank.)

Decide on your minimum dollar value—plane or train ticket, a couple months of food and lodging, emergency fund—and then run with it. It's best to get going, then refine your financial plan as you go. Keep in mind:

- Anyone seeking to pay off loans *while* traveling will likely require a steady income source, too.
- Vagabonding isn't a nonstop vacation. Lying on the beach drinking beer all day every day is going to cost money.
- Long-term travel is not for the faint of heart. Commit. The rest will fall into place.

Once we have saved up some money, it's time to... *not* spend it. How is it possible to travel a year on just a few thousand dollars? In my experience, the below methods are some of the best money-saving techniques out there. I've used all of them at one point or another, and I suggest finding the combination that suits your unique needs and budget.

1. **Go slow.** Transportation is arguably the most expensive part of travel. So minimize it. Pick a country or region, and spend several weeks, months, or an entire year there. No, you won't have as many

patches on your backpack, but you'll have depth, and that's worth quite a bit more. With all the time and money you save by moving more slowly, you could learn a new language, immerse yourself in a different culture, and achieve a nuanced understanding of the place you are in.

Taking eight months to move through Kenya and Zanzibar, I picked up basic Swahili, learned loads about the history, customs, and politics of a region I'd previously known nothing about, and carved a niche for myself in a few places only because I stayed for months. I'll dive much deeper into slow travel in Chapter 5.

2. **Stay flexible.** The more we cling to fixed plans, the more likely we are to spend large sums of money to stick to that perfect itinerary. Uncompromising expectations can lead to overdrawn credit cards and underwhelmed travelers. Rather than setting exact dates on when you must arrive at which destination, consider leaving yourself a window of time (a week, or even a month) to leave space for cheaper transport options and spontaneous opportunities.

3. **Find work trades.** Workaway, Wwoofing, Nu-Mundo, and Helpx are excellent resources to get you started. If you don't have personal contacts in a country (and even if you do) these databases connect willing workers with mutually beneficial trade opportunities. Look for exchanges offering both accommodation and food, or you'll find your money leaking out in daily expenses. Don't be limited by these databases, however. A quick Google search of

"ecolodge/yoga retreat/organic farm + [my destination]" will provide a long list of possible contacts. Craft an email template inquiring about exchanging work for room and board, and send it to your top twenty spots. Only one needs to say yes.

Expect to work four to six hours a day. When you're ready to move on, your current hosts are your best resource. If you have a good rapport, ask them to connect you to their contacts in the next town, city, or country. It helps to have skills—yoga, kitchen, or hospitality experience, web development, marketing, art—that will set you apart from other travelers seeking work exchanges. Don't be shy about emphasizing your strengths; it's not a job application, but it is serious.

I've worked everywhere from farms in Sicily and yoga retreats in Zanzibar to ecolodges in Kenya and guest houses in Cambodia. Where there are tourists, there is work. Where there is work, the thrifty traveler can find a way to earn his or her daily bread.

4. **Take side jobs.** Teach yoga? Give private lessons. Have tech, language, or writing skills? Take on freelance jobs in web design, translation, or editing. Digital platforms like Konversai (a "global knowledge marketplace") also offer user-friendly tools to share all your skills in one-on-one sessions, and make money teaching what you love. Some expenses are unavoidable. Think snacks, toothpaste, metro tickets, snacks, socks, books, snacks… If you're hoping to sustain a nomadic lifestyle long term, at least a little bit of cash income helps. Be sure to

find out what the employment laws for foreigners are in your destination, and try not to break them too blatantly.

If you're interested in working remotely, online resources abound. AngelList, Remote.co, Workew, WeWorkRemotely and Idealist are just the tip of the iceberg. Google "remote work job posting board" and you'll see what I mean. Even today, though, nothing beats word-of-mouth and personal connections. Most of my clients have found me through other clients, referrals from former colleagues, or my published work online. We freelancers and entrepreneurs usually don't have an "off" switch for networking, and are constantly weaving our personal webs of connection. It comes with the territory.

5. **Cook.** Stock up on fresh produce at local markets, and try to prepare most of your own meals (if your trade agreement doesn't include food). Find accommodation with shared kitchen facilities, unless you feel like switching to a fully raw diet. While living in the north of Zanzibar, I mostly lived on cucumbers, tomatoes, mangos, avocados, and eggs. Somehow, those never got old, and I became friends with the local vegetable vendor. In Italy, I frequently choose affordable Airbnb apartments and load up on fresh fruit, cheese, pasta, and olives at the local market. I have consistently found that preparing my own food keeps me grounded and healthy—and less stressed about finances—as I wander.

6. **Prioritize it.** Put sustained exploration at the very top of your list. While traveling, skip the pricey safaris and fancy clubs. Maybe the beer too. Opt out of the posh rooms, coursed meals, and guided adventures that vacationers tend to splurge on. When you're trying to save money before your trip, skip the dinners out, the new clothes, and the latest iPhone; your smoking habit, car, and salon visits can go too. It all adds up. For a long time, I prioritized travel over just about everything so I could afford to go as long as possible. What are you willing to give up for your dream?

Trust. It will work out. Jump. The net will appear. Opportunities you could never have imagined will show up on your path. Try, and see what happens. If or when you decide to go back, most things will be exactly as you left them. I don't think anyone has ever regretted selling everything they own to go travel, but I could be wrong. You can always buy it again and go back home, but the best time to set off on your adventure is always *right now*.

How to Pack One Bag for Life

Packing lists are one of my favorite things to write. Growing up, I would start making my list weeks before family vacations; I started packing pretty far in advance, too. I've stopped making lists—after enough practice, you really don't need them anymore—but I kept the habit of packing far too early.

In 2014, I packed up my sixty-five-liter Osprey back-pack and left the United States for good. Well, more or less. Since then, I've come back to visit friends and family for about a month each year. It would be two years before I added a second small suitcase to my travel kit. Several years ago, when a reader asked me, "What's in your bag?" I had a lot of fun trying to sum up my strategy.

A few caveats: I chase the sun. If you expect your life to include winter, you'll need more warm things. I have my hobbies, and you have yours. Your "extras" will likely be completely different from mine. I leave things, give things away and pick things up near-continuously. It is useful to have friends and family in whose basements, at-tics, and closets you can leave things you don't want to let go of but don't want to carry with you (especially books). It is also useful to get used to giving away something old to make room for something new. Finally, I carry many extraneous items. I suggest it to you, too, even if it's im-practical. It can make the difference between going on vacation and carrying "home" with you.

I wrote this packing list like I write recipes—Italian style, not too specific, and with room for creative inter-pretation. I've split it into logical (to me) sections. Take these as suggestions. You'll invariably find your own list through trial and error.

For when it gets chilly:
- Bright blue wool socks for which your friends will mercilessly mock you
- A shower-resistant outer shell (when it rains, you will wish it were rain-resistant too)

- Bright blue fleece jacket, because there's no such thing as too much turquoise
- Sturdy boots/shoes (I have found trail shoes or trail runners to be ideal)
- A sweater, preferably stolen from a friend

For all the time:
- 1 pair hiking pants
- 1 pair yoga pants
- 1 pair harem pants (also known as Toby pants, if you're in the know!)
- 1 pair jeans/passably normal pants
- X pairs socks and underwear (how many? it depends how often you want to do laundry)
- 5-6 shirts (some for hiking, some for exercise, and some for normal life-ing)
- 1 bathing suit
- Toiletries (pure argan, coconut or almond oil, natural and biodegradable bar soap, toothpaste, toothbrush, tea tree oil, natural deodorant, comb, nail clippers, lip balm, sunblock—that's it!)
- First aid kit (which you will never use but carry around forever "just in case")
- Sunglasses and glasses
- Passport, expired driver's license, bank card, and other assorted bits of paper that sometimes come in handy
- Birkenstock sandals
- Reusable bags (for food shopping, beach day-ing, or hanging on door knobs to look at and wonder why you're carrying so many extra bags)

- Sarong (which serves equally well as scarf, towel, and pillow cover)

For people who likes dresses:
- 1 long skirt
- 2 dresses, neither of which are as practical as they should be, and one bright red

Me-specific things (yours will be different):
- Yoga mat
- Climbing shoes
- Dance shoes
- Books (rotating)
- Notebooks and many, many pens (you will lend them to people and not get them back, so it's good to have 5-10 on hand at any given time)
- Laptop (for work; if you don't work online, maybe skip the laptop—it's a hassle)
- Sleeping bag (and sometimes tent or camping hammock)

Unnecessary but still important things:
- A large quartz crystal
- A large quantity of jewelry
- Smartphone
- Gifts (for people in the next place you're heading)
- Oversized purple headphones
- Smaller-sized purple headphones
- Pretty scarves to put on top of ugly tables

I think packing for long-term travel is more of an art than a science. How can we balance practicality, functionality, comfort, style, and sentimentality in just one bag?

There are as many right answers as there are vagabond-essess. Sometimes you will decide to leave behind some really useful hiking pants to make space for a book you definitely don't need. Sometimes you will gift on a dress that you love to cut down the weight of your bag just another ounce or two. Most likely, you'll get it all wrong at first and end up giving things away in your first destinations, buying handcrafted treasures to replace parts of your wardrobe, and slowly learning the best order to pack in so that the things you need constantly are on the top. There's no point digging into all those details; in time you'll find a system that works for you.

Intuitive Trip-Planning

In 2015, I moved to Cape Town, South Africa for a while. I did not know anyone there. I did not have a plan or a very good explanation of why I wanted to go. I had met a lot of South Africans while traveling in East Africa, and Cape Town had come up several times in conversation. Somehow, like Zanzibar before it, the idea lodged itself in my subconscious and stayed there. As I prepared to leave Zanzibar, feeling un-characteristically vague and directionless, a small voice in my gut whispered, "Cape Town. Cape Town. Cape Town."

So I reached out to two South African friends with Cape Town connections who connected me to other friends in the area with houses to rent, people to meet, or helpful sugges-tions to smooth my landing. After a stop in the U.S. to visit family and regroup, I set off for South Africa via Amsterdam and Sicily—a circuitous route which, I swear, made perfect sense at the time. I ended up falling in love with the city, the mountains, the ocean, and the people. I would proceed to spend most of the next year living there.

Moving to Costa Rica in 2017 was another instance of successful intuitive trip-planning. I had been accepted to three master's programs—one in Vermont, one in London, and one in Costa Rica. Each was highly attractive to me for different reasons. Each location had its appeal too. Yet, I knew—I really knew, underneath the weeks of wishy-washy deliberation—that Costa Rica was the right choice. Of course, I listened to that knowing, and I'm still here.

Whenever we have a decision to make, there is a part of us (call it intuition, gut instinct, whatever you will) that knows the "right" answer before our brain does. We can arrive at it by logic, weighing the pros and cons, asking a dozen people for advice, and reading through piles of travel guides. Or, we can skip the winding road of rational decision-making and hop straight to our destination: what feels right *is* right.

You argue, but this is how drug addicts, hedonists, and psychiatric patients are made—acting on impulse. I counter, impulse is not the same as intuition. I sat with my decision to head to Cape Town for nearly two weeks before buying tickets. I reconsidered all my other options, gave logic its chance to sort through the possibilities. But my intuition didn't waver: *Warm air, ocean tides—a chance to learn to surf, finally!—and hiking trails, even horses, and then all the things a city can offer: a blank slab of the unknown where you can inscribe the next months of this adventure word by novel word.* I have never regretted listening to that inner voice of absolute knowing.

The unknown and intuition are particularly enmeshed for me. What feels "right," more often than not, is whatever appears most shrouded in mystery. My gut has a deep love affair with the yet-to-be-revealed of a new culture, new community, new dance, new sport, new path, new chance. Of course, that is my "what feels right," and I neither suggest nor expect it should be the same for you. It is only interesting and instructive to note where our intuition points us time and time again. Does your intuition keep urging you back to the same place no matter how many times you leave? There is information there; pay attention, and you may learn something about yourself and your path. Has your intuition been screaming at you to try a new city, *any city*? If you listen, maybe there is insight to be gained about the place you are now and why it isn't right for you.

When we hold a question in our mind's hands, turning it this way and that, asking *where, who, what, when, and most of all, why*—what is the first voice to answer, and what does it say? Say hello to your intuition, because that's who's speaking! I suggest following this voice as you plan your trips. There is a place on the map singing a siren song just for you. That is where you should go. Don't plan too far ahead, because the tune may change, a voice may whisper, "Zanzibar," and you may want to tear up your whole itinerary and veer off into unanticipated territories. Don't fill your days with too many "musts" and "shoulds," and instead leave time for the irresistible, spontaneous possibilities that arise unexpectedly and for which we can never properly plan ahead.

> "Go confidently in the direction of your dreams. Live the life you have imagined."
> —Henry David Thoreau

Healthcare

While living in Cape Town, I woke up one morning with intense pain in one wisdom tooth. When I looked in the mirror I didn't know whether to laugh or cry; one side of my face had swollen up to extreme chipmunk proportions.

I panicked.

I did not have insurance in South Africa. I did not have a dentist. I didn't even know where to start, and it was hard to think with so much pain in my jaw.

After a few deep breaths and a few phone calls, however, I had an appointment at a nearby dental clinic. A few days later, after the antibiotics kicked in and the infection went down, I returned for a straightforward extraction. Incidentally, the whole process cost less than a simple dental check-up in the U.S.

While on a surf retreat in Portugal, I similarly panicked when faced with a new, inexplicable pain in my left ovary. I held back tears while I struggled through a phone call with a hospital in Porto with my very basic Portuguese to book an appointment for an ultrasound. Fortunately, the doctor who examined me spoke flawless English and more or less eased my worries and balanced out my lively, worst-case-scenario imagination. A follow-up appointment a few months later in the U.S. would reveal a benign cyst of no concern.

———

Getting sick while traveling alone is anxiety-inducing. I'm not going to sugarcoat it. More than anxiety-inducing, it is unsettling to navigate a foreign healthcare system alone, especially if you don't speak the language. It is lonely to be bedridden with no close friends or family to rub your back or bring you tea. It is uncomfortable, for so many reasons, to be violently ill in a hostel dormitory or homestay.

Minor health complications will invariably arise, however. To put it bluntly, the vagabondess just sucks it up and figures it out. Or she feels sorry for herself for a while, and then sucks it up and deals with it. Google and friends are good resources when the situation calls for clinics and appointments. We'll get into health and wellness, including practical preventative care on the road, in much greater detail in Chapter 6. For now, I'll just say that travel insurance is generally recommended. I have recently signed on with digital nomad insurance Safety-Wing. While filing claims is arguably just as stressful as paying out of pocket for services in places where healthcare is affordable, accidents happen, and covering your bases in the event of an emergency is the sensible thing to do.

Everything Else

> "I want all the cultures of all lands to be blown about my house as freely as possible. But I refuse to be blown off my feet by any."
> —Mahatma Gandhi

I am not going to make recommendations for gear. No one is paying me to do that, and I think just about anything you pick up at your local outfitter will be just fine. Now, if you're thinking of distance walking, invest in a great backpack and shoes. It's worth it. If you're planning to camp regularly in extreme conditions, invest in a great tent. Otherwise, whatever you already have on hand will probably work out. If it doesn't, you'll figure that out along the way and adapt.

I also won't tell you that you must learn the language of the country where you'll be traveling. That said, if you think you'll be sticking around for a while, I encourage you to try. Apps like Duolingo, Mondly, Konversai, and Babbel have brought language learning into the twenty-first century, making it fun, accessible, and affordable. My number one rule of learning a language: Don't be afraid to sound stupid! You'll sound like a two-year-old throwing a tantrum for a long time. Who cares? Most people will appreciate that you're even trying. Some will laugh at you. Again, who cares? You're doing a great thing for your brain; learning a language is one of the absolute best actions you can take to improve neuroplasticity. What's more, by truly making an effort to communicate in your host culture's language, you're doing a favor to the reputation of tourists everywhere. Even learning to say

51

"hello," "how are you?" "please," and "thank you" goes a long way.

Regardless of the length of your visit, it is an excellent idea to read up a bit on the culture and customs of any place you'll be landing for the first time. What is appropriate dress for women? How do people greet one another? What horribly rude gaffs do tourists tend to make? Is it offensive to point the soles of your feet at someone (Tibet), leave your hair uncovered (much of the Muslim world, particularly in any place of worship), or make eye contact (China)? Is direct communication appreciated, or are subtlety and tact the rule? A vacationer may not care about these things, but a vagabondess seeks to move through unfamiliar spaces with grace and respect. Doing a bit of research ahead of time can make this a much easier feat to achieve.

No one expects foreigners to achieve cultural fluency immediately, but they should expect us to try. We don't have to agree with it. We don't have to like it. But the fact of the matter is that when we are guests in another place and culture, we don't get to make the rules. To me, this is *the* core value of ethical travel: *It's not up to me.* I chose to travel to a place where women are expected to dress modestly, so I had better be prepared to dress modestly. I chose to visit a place where eating with the left hand is dirty, so you're damn right I'm going to eat with my right hand. I chose to live in a culture where no one is ever on time; I may never get used to it, but I take responsibility for putting myself into a cultural context that challenges my deeply embedded punctuality. I'll delve much deeper into personal boundaries in Chapter 8. For now, suffice it to say that if the customs of my destination are in fundamental violation of my personal boundaries, then perhaps I should choose a different destination.

It is impossible to be perfectly prepared for all outcomes (although with time and practice you may come close). And unless you're into extreme sports or survival camping, you really don't need to be perfectly prepared. Your survival does not depend on it. Be prepared to mess up, forget things, fail to communicate clearly, offend, and be offended. Be prepared to feel scared, lonely, confused, aimless, and silly. Be prepared to be very uncomfortable. Be prepared to struggle. Be prepared to be hopelessly unprepared. Be prepared to get it wrong. The rest is incidental.

This goes for all of the above categories. You don't have to get it all right right from the start. You'll make mistakes. You'll curse your former self for forgetting to pack a raincoat. You'll screw your future self over by leaving your toothbrush behind at every single hostel. You'll be cold, wet, hungry, and stressed, all thanks to your imperfect preparations.

And you know what? I think that's exactly as it should be. Stress has always, always been an inconsequential—yet paradoxically fundamental—footnote to my travels. Bumbling through Italy, utterly lost; wandering the streets of Istanbul with my best friend, utterly lost; scouring Kolkata for a guest house alone, utterly lost. Anxiously running to catch trains; bartering for taxis, tuk tuks, motorcycles, often walking instead in stubborn frustration; searching for addresses, waiting for rides or fruitlessly seeking a quiet corner to regroup, adrenaline saturating my blood.

None of it is fun, per se. Most of it gets pushed to the sidelines of our rose-toned memories of blissful voyages and wild adventures. But it is all travel. That stress means we are stretching the limits of our comfort zone, expanding boundaries, and pushing ourselves to be both stronger and more pliant. I certainly don't like it; I've never been into adrenaline, and as the years pass, I become more and more averse to discomfort for the sake of discomfort. My stress management toolkit is fairly sparse, and sometimes I allow anxiety to get the best of me. Nonetheless, I continue to believe that stress should be a manageable, eventually forgettable, part of travel.

If travel isn't just a little stressful at times—and all-out infuriating at others—then what is it? Because if it's too easy, then it isn't challenging; and if it isn't challenging, then we're not learning or growing as much as we could. So don't worry about getting everything right. You'll be better off embracing the whole stressful, blissful, kaleidoscopic emotional rollercoaster as you embark on your journey.

STRUGGLE: A TRAVEL MANIFESTO

If you travel (or live) where the mother tongue is not your mother tongue, you will struggle. The mundane will become complex and challenging, and you will no longer take your habitual fluency in the everyday for granted.

This is a good thing.

It shouldn't be easy. It is through challenge, discomfort, dis-ease that we grow best. So, this is my travel manifesto for you.

Go out into the world, and struggle:

Struggle, to purchase underwear.
Struggle, to ask directions.
Struggle, to talk about the things that matter to you.

Comprehending the cost of your coffee will be a minor victory.
Catching a compliment on the first go will be cause for celebration.
Navigating a simple interaction will thrill you—as it never could at home.

These are all very good things.

For it should not be easy, this day-to-day living.
It should not be easy, this being in the world.

So struggle, to take the bus.
And struggle, to order at the bar.

Struggle, to understand.
Struggle, to say you have understood.

For it should not be easy, this everyday living.
It should not be easy, this quotidian life thing.

When it is easy, we forget—

We forget that buying our coffee is in fact a minor
victory,
that a compliment is cause for celebration,
that understanding is a miracle,
and being understood doubly so.
So struggle,
and don't forget
that it is a privilege to move through this world with
grace.

And when you do forget,
as, invariably, we do,

Go out again
and travel.

Remember what it feels like
to struggle for the simplest of rewards.
Remember not to take
anything for granted.
Remember how to move
through this world
with grace.

III. Trust

Say Hello to Your Intuition

"The intuitive mind is a sacred gift and the rational mind is a faithful servant. We have created a society that honours the servant and has forgotten the gift."—Albert Einstein

To TRUST A STRANGER IS A radically subversive act in a world that tells us to fear the other.

If I reach back in my memory, I trace one of my first acts of irrational trust to my time living in Paris.

The year is 2009. The setting: A nighttime picnic with a friend beneath the Eiffel Tower, eating cheese and baguette, and drinking red wine straight from the bottle.

We meet a couple of French guys around our age, here for the same reason: to drink the Parisian night air and breathe the city's spirit of elegant freedom. We practice our French, answer the usual questions, share stories and wine. As the evening draws to a close, one of our new friends offers me a ride home on his motorcycle.

Ali is a stranger. I am a very young woman living alone in Paris. All conventional narratives around strangers and safety scream caution. I accept.

The ensuing drive through the midnight city streets is more intoxicating than any bottle of wine has ever been. The streetlights and headlights blur into neon lines, stretching motion into something visible. The wind blows my hair across my eyes. It tastes like elegant freedom. Nothing exists but this moment of wild, wildly subversive trust in my fellow human, in the universe, in the darkness, in perpetual movement.

There is no dramatic climax to this story. Ali drops me off at my doorstep, and the night ends there. And yet, perhaps something has shifted that night. I have tasted a drug far more addictive than anything chemical. I have tasted trust, laced with freedom, and I'll spend the next ten years seeking my fix.

In a world that expects the worst, I believe offering the best of ourselves is a fundamental act of radical subversion.

In a society that sees mal-intent, hate, danger and selfishness everywhere—with or without due cause—what is more rebellious than goodwill, love, and trust toward our fellow human beings?

None of us controls what the world gives to us—hate or love, malcontent or goodwill—yet each of us decides what we offer in return.

Rebellion, sometimes, is a broad smile. Subversion, maybe, is the wide open arms of anyone who chooses love and trust in this crazy world.

Faith isn't always about an intangible entity in the heavens; sometimes, it is about the flesh and blood reality all around us. Just like religious faith, the faith of a vagabondess colors her experience of the entire world, gives meaning to the mundane, and elevates her spirits in moments of doubt. The optimism that threads through my travels is a system of belief in itself. So let's talk about trust—and intuition.

Trust

> "Trust in dreams, for in them is the hidden gate to eternity."—Kahlil Gibran

In this age of fake news and post-truth skepticism, trust is perhaps one of the rarest and most valuable currencies out there. At least in U.S. society, we are conditioned to mistrust strangers, to look on anything "other" with suspicion, and even to doubt our own minds. Trust is the foundation of human relationships, and yet, so often we withhold it because the rational mind sees danger everywhere. Without it, however, we divorce our existence from the complex web of connections that give our lives structure and support.

How can we embrace it, then? We can start by studying and ultimately integrating into our lives the following three levels of trust:

- Trust in self.
- Trust in others.
- Trust in the Universe.

Trusting ourselves isn't a platitude; rather, it is a fierce commitment to that soft inner voice that speaks from our gut and is just about always right. It is a promise: "I hear you. I value you. I follow you." Trust in self doesn't grow overnight, especially if we've spent a lifetime inculcated in the fallacy that everyone else knows more about our needs and desires than we do. Nonetheless, I believe we must cultivate an unshakeable trust in our own voice of intuition if we are to successfully set off on a solo adventure.

Any kind of mindfulness practice that brings awareness to the body and breath is a good way to hone listening skills and connect to that inner voice. Martial arts or other physical training that builds physical and mental strength can further support confidence in a strong mind and body and their capacity to carry us anywhere. Most importantly, we must commit to listening; trust will naturally follow in its own time. No one will hold us accountable to this commitment, yet it is critical to a successful cultivation of self-trust. The promise is this: *I will listen. I will listen to my inner voice. I will listen to my body. And if I can't hear, I will work harder to open my ears. I will listen.*

Trust in others, as discussed above, is an act of rebellion, subversion, and faith. We choose to trust others; we don't wait for proof that they can be trusted. In fact, we choose to trust them *in spite of proof that they cannot be trusted.* Logic declares that there is never enough proof. They may have kept their word this time, but what about next time? They say I can trust them, but the last person who said that broke my trust. People will disappoint us. They will break our trust. They will cause us to doubt the wisdom of trusting again, opening again, letting ourselves be vulnerable again.

True trust in others—especially strangers—cannot arise from naivete or blind innocence. To the contrary, it must grow from complex awareness of the good and the bad in humanity, acceptance of that duality, and finally a conscious decision to *trust anyway.* I call it optimism. Rebellion against cynicism. How many times have I been disappointed by the men I date? Too many to count. How many times have I accepted a Facebook friend request from a stranger only to block them a few days later after they surpassed the acceptable level of harassment? Hundreds. (The acceptable amount of harassment is zero, by the way.) How often have friends, self-defense students, and news media described in harrowing detail all the ways in which people are not to be trusted? Every goddamn day.

It would be easy to build up walls, withdraw into a hard, safe shell, hide behind wizened cynicism. But I do not want to do that. I keep dating. I keep talking to strangers (real and virtual). I keep holding space for the stories that break my heart while believing the day will come where we have different stories to tell. My optimism is not primarily about the future, however; it is about the here and now.

I am an optimist not because I do not see the darkness (of course I do—who could ignore it?), but because I choose to always strive for its opposite. The world is at war; I hope for peace. Humans are cruel, petty, hateful, and foolish, but I believe—I know—they are more often kind, generous, loving, and wise. No matter how many times I encounter the former, I continue to trust. This is not naïveté; it is optimism. My world—the world I want to live in—must deserve my faith.

How can we be incorrigible optimists in a world that is constantly turning on its head? Simple. We choose it. There is no other way.

Finally, we have trust in the Universe. Difficult to dissect without falling into the snare of new-age truisms, but I'll try. Call it whatever you want: The Universe. The Divine. Spirit. God. Fate. Luck. It's out there, and it has a hand in the seemingly illogical twists and turns of our life path. It is an act of supreme faith to jump into the air, trusting that the hand of fate will appear and catch us. Quit the job. Sell the house. End the relationship. Leave the country. Fill in the blank with the thing you are afraid to do but know you must do, because the wind of change has touched your face and you can't ignore it.

For me, that "fill in the blank" has manifested as ending a long-term relationship, quitting a good, stable job as an editor, jumping off a bridge with a bungee cord attached to my ankles, sticking my thumb out on a Croatian highway, moving into my friend's attic in Helsinki with no clear action plan, and countless other leaps into the ether. It has manifested, too, in beginning projects with no financial backing, opening my heart to new connections, and moving to new countries because the wind told me to.

It is always terrifying to do *that* thing. But without this trust and surrender, we will find it difficult to open to the spontaneous blessings of solo travel. A vagabondess trusts the wind when it sings, "Jump. I will teach you how to fly." And she is rarely disappointed.

Be advised: The net that appears when we leap does not always look the way we expect or desire. The Universe doesn't always give us what we want; however (and this is one platitude I fully embrace), She does give us the lessons we need.

We build up these "one big thing," "fill-in-the-blank" moments of change so much. Yet, I've found that the *idea* of the thing is often scarier than the thing itself. Take performing, for instance. Soon after moving to Costa Rica in 2017, I started an open mic night at a popular local bar and restaurant. I had only recently started playing guitar and writing songs, and even more recently begun to share those songs with anyone other than the monkeys outside my house. Nerves kept my heart beating double-time and my eyes wide open the night before the event. Jitters about singing had me over-awake and on high alert.

Fear is usually scarier than its object. Those symptoms began to recede almost instantly once I got up on stage. The thing itself—a room packed with friendly, vaguely interested people—was not nearly as nerve-wracking as the *idea* of performing. And so the adrenaline (fueled by fear, as it always is) seeped away. My body returned to stasis.

So we jump. We trust. We overcome, transcend, and the question becomes, *now what*? I suppose we keep doing it. We keep overcoming, confronting, trusting, transcending until the real object of our fear—the idea of the thing—no longer exists, and only the thing itself remains.

Intuition

> "Practice listening to your intuition, your inner voice; ask questions; be curious; see what you see; hear what you hear; and then act upon what you know to be true. These intuitive powers were given to your soul at birth."—Clarissa Pinkola Estés

They say that our brains only *consciously* process about 10% of the information we receive through our senses—sight, sound, smell, taste, touch. (I read it in a book about neuroscience, so it must be at least vaguely rooted in fact.) What happens to that other 90%? I believe (and I'm not alone) that this unprocessed information that enters our brains yet never filters into conscious awareness becomes our "intuition," "sixth sense," or "gut feeling." We know so much more than we think we know. We don't even know how much we truly know.

Intuition doesn't receive the accolades it deserves, and yet, it can save a life. People have avoided potentially fatal assaults because their intuition told them something "wasn't right" about a situation, a person, a place. Survivors of natural disasters have found their way to safety through pure instinct. Drop a person into the woods, and with minimal survival training, they will find a way through. We are the product of millions of years of evolution, which has both blessed and cursed us with certain biological quirks.

The "lizard brain" that resides in our amygdala governs our flight, fight, or freeze response, either saving our lives when we nearly step on a poisonous snake or sending us into a panic attack when the doorbell rings.

Instinct and intuition are, I believe, closely linked. What is intuition, if not something deeper and more ancient than intellect or reason speaking from our lizard core, instructing us to fight, run, or freeze? Certainly, there are times when our inner reptile is in dissonance with the modern world; we do not need to run away from fireworks, and we definitely should not freeze in oncoming traffic. Our traumas are often the product of this dissonance between ancient coping mechanisms and modern challenges. We are more than our instincts, of course. That is what makes us human, or so claim at least a few spiritual disciplines. Nonetheless, this embodied animal wisdom can also bring us through the woods unscathed, physically and metaphorically. It is a proven technology to be respected, developed, and used with discernment.

In the case of solo travel, a finely tuned intuition is a vagabondess' most important tool for surviving, thriving, and transforming in the unfamiliar. There is no need for a detailed guide for where to go, who to trust, or how to get around if you truly tap into the source of wisdom that resides in your own brilliant gut.

In 2013, I spent five days sharing a hotel room with a fellow traveler I had met on the bus to Phnom Penh. We wandered barefoot through the city (don't ask), made meals of the free peanuts that came with our cold, fifty-cent beer, laughed a lot, and... that was it. I never felt unsafe or uncomfortable in the tiny room we shared. He never crossed any lines. I knew—my intuition knew—that this was someone good, someone I could trust. Some of that other 90% of unprocessed information must have given me the clues I needed to make the call. You could call it luck, except I have hundreds of stories like this one. So does every vagabondess I know. I have to believe that intuition has something to do with it.

Intuition can save your life, get you back to your hostel when you're lost in a new city, and tell you which new friends deserve your trust. Here are a few simple ways to hone it:

- Spend time walking around barefoot. The soles of our feet are as receptive to tactile information as the palms of our hands. We close off that source when we constantly cover our feet.

- Close your eyes, and listen with your other senses. "You have to see it to believe it" has become the adage of our times. Yet smell, taste, touch, and sound can provide us with just as much information as our eyes—if not more. The problem is, we tune out from those channels when we focus all our awareness on *seeing*.

- Choose a somatic practice—dance, yoga, martial arts, anything!—that gets you out of your brain and into your body. *Body wisdom* is very real; one of the best ways to channel it is through movement practices that let the body speak.

- Find your flow in a creative process. Be it painting, writing, singing, playing music, cooking, or crafting, a creative practice where you can truly find your flow state also teaches you to drop out of your head and into another wavelength of being, doing, and knowing. It is by spending time on these other levels of connection with self and the world that we learn the language of our intuition.

- Practice listening to your body in small ways. Eat when you're hungry. Stretch when your muscles are tight. Allow spontaneous movement, sound, and breath to move through you without filtering or analyzing. Leave a location when it feels unsafe. Speak up when touch, words, or actions feel violent. Intuition is a language we all speak, but it gets rusty without use, like any language. When we practice listening to and honoring the body's wisdom, we absorb a key message: *My intuition is here, and it is valuable.*

- Reflect. Sift through memories for clues to your intuition. When has it spoken clearly in the past? What happened when you listened? What happened when you didn't listen. Where do you feel intuition speaking in your body? Taking time to research our personal history of successes can provide us with valuable self-awareness, making it easier to recognize and trust our intuition in the future.

An important caveat: Discernment is absolutely vital. A large array of factors like trauma, technology, outside manipulation, and low self-esteem can cloud our intuition, and sometimes even twist it inside out. I am usually right about the people and places I choose, but I've been wrong a handful of times. That's why practice is so important.

The more time we spend listening to our inner voice, and the more times we act accordingly, the more accurate our intuition becomes. The more we practice, the lower the risk of falling for false signals posing as intuition.

So then, where should you go? What should you do? How will you know who to trust, whom to talk to, where to stay, how to live? You already have all of the answers to all of these questions. The hard part is learning how to hear them. Silence helps, so let's talk about that delicate balance between speech and silence, socializing and solitude, in Chapter 4.

———

GIVE ME LONELINESS

Give me loneliness.
Give me long mornings where not one word passes my lips.
Give me dinner for one.
Give me the sweet melancholy of looking out at the sea and whispering—only for myself—"that is so fucking beautiful."

Beauty shared doubles in its charms,
but beauty held within multiplies without bounds.

Give me loneliness.
Give me empty roads in forgotten towns.
Give me shadowless landscapes where my soul can dance all alone.
Give me sleep, because there is nothing—no one—for which to stay awake.
Give me dreams of open skies and towering cliffs and violent surf, which do not fade on waking.
Give me a soft shawl of solitude, with a bittersweet border.
Let me wrap myself in it for an hour, a week, or a year, to keep my dreams warm in daytime.

Dreams shared may reach towering heights for a while,
but dreams kept inside—these grow wings in their own right.

Give me loneliness.
Give me a short coffee and a long, long morning.
Give me voices on the breeze that require no answer.
Give me the low, mournful song of no footsteps passing.

Give me loneliness—
When I am ready
…after a while…
I will look up and smile.
And you will understand that I was never lonely
not really
but only warming my dreams over a silent flame,
biding my time
until the wind was right
to turn whispers
into flight.

IV. Solitude & Socializing

Introverting on the Extrovert's Path

Hermit Day: I stare resolutely out the window of my Uber at the windy Cape Town scene, quite determined to see that any attempts at conversation die a quick death.

Social Day: I sit down on the train from Istanbul, Turkey to Sofia, Bulgaria and immediately strike up a conversation with the French couple sharing my compartment. It feels good to have any words whatsoever coming out of my mouth after a solid twenty-four hours of alone time.

Hermit Day 2: Our fellow hostel guest in Matosinhos, Portugal is a kind man from Tokyo determined to talk about marijuana at length. While he engages my friend in discussion about alternative cures for cancer, I stare resolutely at my book, quite determined to leave the onus of politeness on her.

Social Day 2: I walk into a bar in Bangkok alone. Within thirty minutes, I have a table full of new friends, one guy's phone number in my pocket, and a place to stay, should I ever find myself in Munich.

Hermit Day 3: A talkative-looking chap sits down next to me at a cafe. I pretend not to speak English, or Portuguese, or French, or Spanish… I stare resolutely at my coffee cup, quite determined to be Russian for the next hour or so.

Social Day 3: I sit down next to a stranger in a cafe and say hello. Somehow, we're best friends after an hour and I've invited them to a party I'm throwing that night.

———

TRAVEL WILL CHALLENGE YOU, no matter where you land on the introvert-extrovert spectrum. Openness does not make sense without closedness. No one can be "on" all the time, despite the well-worn cliché of the inexhaustibly garrulous solo traveler. For permanent vagabonds, this can be a slow realization. After all, aren't curiosity, openness, and willingness to engage the key ingredients to meaningful travel experiences? Of course. But then, so is balance.

Myth: You have to be an extrovert to be a solo traveler.

I love my alone time like a dog with a bone. I will fight you for it. I am probably less social, less inclined to long chats, and less of a people person than you are (and I don't know who you are). I can write until my fingers fall off about kindness, talking to strangers, being open to the world, and all of those beautiful values that I truly believe define a vagabondess. Yet, to paint you a fair picture of this lifestyle, I would be remiss if I did not also mention selfishness, ignoring talkative strangers, and withdrawing from the world.

One need not be endlessly friendly, happy, and social in order to be a successful vagabondess. I can assure you I am not. I like to think of a long-term solo journey as a kind of free-form soup. You gather your ingredients—reading, writing, and thinking; yoga and meditation; bizarre and fascinating interactions with strangers; learning experiences of all ilk; wordless (heart-centered) communication with people and spaces; silence; dancing and movement; kindness; sadness; curiosity; introspection; creativity; play; adventure. You add a dash of this and a spoonful of that. You stir in the exact amount of each ingredient that *you* want to taste in your soup experience (it is just for you). Let simmer. Wait patiently for all the flavors to get to know each other. And finally, savor.

Your travel soup will not look or taste the same as mine. However, I believe that most of us need the following ingredients in our journey, in varying quantities: solitude, silence, socializing, community, and loneliness.

Solitude

2015, Sicily, Italy

The wind picks up, rifling the pages of my journal with a sharp, snapping sound. The waves inch closer, threatening to flood my hideaway beneath a dock. I hear birds, distant voices, but I am very much alone in this moment. I drink in the delicious breeze on my skin—the rare moment of true quiet—and I smile. It is a smile no one will see, and all the more precious for being mine alone.

The moment is exquisite. Free of the obligation to smile at, respond to, or engage with presences outside of myself, I turn these actions inward. I smile to smile, I answer my own voice, and I hug my own knees to my chest. It is a particular shade of joy that I feel. Not the vibrant, trembling joy of love. Not the bright and shiny joy of adventure. This is a softer, subtler, self-effacing hue that nestles deep within my own core, always.

When I take the time to seek solitude, I remember that joy is there. The wind and water dissolve the tenuous strands of forgetting coiled around it. No matter how much my relationships with others may nourish me, they can never give me what their absence bestows: Empty space in which to grow. Deep quiet in which to hear my own voice. A precious moment of "nothing-else-ness" wherein I may truly understand the "something" that I alone inhabit. I still exist in solitude.

Every one of us exists in solitude. We are expansive, stunningly alive, and humming with words and music. To recognize that existence, outside of its relationship to other human existences, is powerful indeed. How profound a teacher this solitude proves itself to be each time I sit in its classroom! Ten minutes of "nothing-else" seem to offer more inspiration than hours of "something."

In solitude, you exist in your entirety, dear vagabondess. This is a lesson I hope you will learn on your solo journeys, if you do not know it already.

It's June of 2019, and I've booked myself a week in a remote bed and breakfast in the mountains of Liguria, Italy. The owner is a gruff, unsocial man around my age. The other guests are couples with exacting vacation itineraries and little time to sit around. In the mornings, I wander the countryside looking for public hiking trails and stumbling upon private vineyards instead. I spend my evenings playing guitar and writing poetry on the checkered terrace of the villa, watching the late summer sun cast long shadows over the valley below. I make one trip into town for groceries, then proceed to spend an indulgent amount of time in self-imposed solitude.

I need it. I've been visiting with dear friends and family nonstop for two months, and my social tank is running on empty. I am craving quiet, emptiness, space. I'm craving it desperately. My inner world has become a tangled jungle of unconsidered thoughts and feelings; I haven't had time to simply sit with my own head in... weeks! If I didn't get this break from people, I'd be suffering the same symptoms as a workaholic on vacation: stress, headaches, irritability, irrational anger, and misdirected frustration. The introverts out there will know what I mean.

Someone once told me that I like the idea of people more than I actually like people, and he was probably right. Humans are so fascinating! Culture, language, food, stories—I love it, and I want to soak it all in about 50% of the time. The other 50%, I cherish my own company, and I don't want to share it.

For those naturally inclined to solitude, there's a spider-web-fine line—at which you may stare resolutely while seeking to avoid conversation—between comfortable, uncompromising introspection and exhausting, unrelenting openness. And if you can dangle from that line by your toes in an incredible feat of mental acrobatics you just might find the recipe for richly balanced, joyful adventure.

Solo travel is a bit of a misnomer; you often have to try—hard—to truly be alone. New friends are waiting at hostels, on trains, in cafes, at the beach, in the grocery store—*everywhere*. It would be kind of creepy if they weren't so well-intentioned. If you are traveling alone and clearly foreign, everyone will want to know your story and keep you company. If you are a woman traveling alone, this is doubly true.

I generally find it best to heed the call to hermitage when it comes. There is nothing worse than insincere friendliness, and I was never much good at acting. While solitude does not come automatically with solo travel, there are many ways to find it. My favorites include:

- Renting an affordable Airbnb studio rather than snagging the cheapest bed in a hostel dormitory where you will never, ever be alone.
- Literally disappearing into the woods for a few days for some solo hiking or camping.
- Learning how to set clear boundaries. ("To be honest, I'm not feeling like having a conversation right now. Thank you for understanding!" feels awkward

at first, but can work wonders for avoiding social burnout.)

- Sitting alone at a cafe or restaurant with a good book or journal. There is a particular sweetness to solitude in crowds, which we can taste in busy public spaces.

- Walking through a city or town alone without listening to music or doing anything to block out the surrounding chaos. Becoming an observer—a pair of legs with eyes, nose, and ears—can bring us into a state of witness, sitting on the edge of a spectacle, both alone and involved in what we are witnessing.

Silence

This may sound odd coming from a writer, but words are not the only way to communicate. In fact, I'm not even sure they're the best way to communicate. Movement is a powerful language, often more honest than any verbal idiom. Five minutes of eye contact can reveal more than an hour of conversation. Everything speaks to us—trees, animals, city lights, a subtle angling of the neck, wind and rain—but we're usually too busy chatting to hear any of it.

Silence has its own vocabulary, which the solo traveler will likely come to know well in times of solitude, rest, or transition: A tilt of the head. The kiss of hot sand on bare feet. The hollow echo of an empty room. The hum of a blank page. It is music in its own right. You decide if the melody is sad or joyful... or exquisitely both.

If you want to immerse yourself in this music for a few days, you might consider a *Vipassana* meditation retreat.

From three to ten days of silent meditation, a *Vipassana* experience will challenge even the most taciturn among us. (For an immersion into solitude, I have found nothing more intense than the vision quest model: a three- or four-day solo fast in the wilderness. No food, no company, and nothing to do for four days—nothing else will feel quite so solitary after that.) Stripping away the trappings of our quotidian existence, we become better versed in subtler modes of communication and expression.

There is not so much to say about silence, really. To carry on about it would defy its very nature. Just remember: you exist in the absence of speech or expression, and in the absence of other humans with whom to share it. From time to time, the sound of that pure existence is honey to overstimulated ears.

Social Time

November, 2009, Paris

I'm eighteen, and Paris is home for the year. It's a chilly night, ten or eleven o'clock. I've just gotten off the metro somewhere in the center of the city.

The text messages, which don't yet reach underground, arrive in a flurry. "Can't make it." "Running late. Might bail." "May come later. Not sure."

Well, shit. I'm not going in there alone. My first instinct is to flee right back the way I came. But then I glance at the bar—warmly lit wood and brass, clientele dressed in the ultra-chic black uniform of the city—and my natural stubborn streak takes over. So what if no one else is coming? It's

Friday night, and it took me forty-five minutes to get here. I'll be damned if I go home without at least checking out the scene.

I open the door. Step into the warm light. Rest an elbow on the narrow wooden bar. Order a glass of wine—white, I think. Before long, someone strikes up a conversation. I practice my French. Find that it comes easily with strangers, without pressure. Somehow I find myself at a table with a dozen young people from the south of France. Celebrating—a birthday, I think.

The evening flows, and I leave for home many hours later, glowing with perverse satisfaction more than anything. I went out alone, and it didn't suck. So there, world!

That night in Paris was, in a way, a pivotal moment in my solo travel career. It's one thing to hop on a train alone, sightsee alone, or even eat at a restaurant alone. We might do all of these things with ease, yet panic at the thought of entering a bar or club without backup. And by "we" I especially mean "we women."

Why? Why is this the impassable limit of independence? We've had it drilled into our heads that this simply is not done. That old fear rhetoric strikes again. Creepy guys, lechy guys, drunk guys; social stigma, weird looks, pitying stares; feeling lonely, awkward, unpopular, uncomfortable…

Forget it. We're convinced. Let's never go out alone. Except, reality is better than our imagination—and certainly better than our nightmares. I went to bed that November night in Paris feeling empowered. "Not sucking" may seem like a low bar for an evening out, but when we're conditioned to expect utter disaster from any solo foray into social activity, "not sucking" is actually a high achievement.

In the years since, I've often gone to pubs, live music shows, dance clubs, bars, and festivals alone. Sometimes I even—*gasp*—prefer it. The key is usually to keep expectations low or non-existent. If you'll happily go home disappointed, a nice evening out is a pleasant surprise. Leaving expectations at home, we can then open naturally to possibile connections with our fellow humans. Of course, it's important to stay fairly sober, prepared to deflect the creepy ones who defy national and personal boundaries, and aware of our surroundings.

Finally, we just have to go. *Just do the thing, whatever it is.* This is your new travel mantra. Worrying about it, stressing about it, agonizing over it—none of these thought ruts will make it any easier. Open the door. Step inside. Order a glass of wine, a cup of coffee, or nothing at all. Smile. Say hello to a stranger. It's not such a big deal, after all, and there will be plenty of time to go back to your solitude later.

Worst case scenario? It's terrible, you go home, and you can blame me later for even suggesting such a thing. Best case scenario? You learn that you truly can do anything, because you're a badass, and because life isn't as scary as everyone tells you. (Of course, you can always stay in a hostel, book a room in an Airbnb, or stay with a Couchsurfing host, and then the social time will be inevitable and straightforward.)

You don't have to be an extrovert to be a solo traveler, because anyone *can* cultivate boldness, friendliness, and social confidence. I don't really believe in the whole introvert-extrovert dichotomy, anyway, at least not the way it's presented nowadays. We can all break out of our shell. We can all choose to be social, sometimes.

These days, I regularly present workshops to anywhere from twenty to fifty people, record live videos on social media that reach thousands, and get up on stage to share poetry or music. But I haven't always been so bold. As I remember it, I was a shy, cautious, and quiet little girl. In high school, I limped painfully through public speaking assignments.

I credit my years of solo travel with this transformation (or perhaps expansion) of my personality. Each time I surpass my preconceived "limits," every time I push the boundaries of my so-called "comfort zone," I learn that limits are illusory and comfort is learned. That is why "feel the fear and do it anyway" is one of my favorite maxims. It works. It doesn't mean "ignore your instincts," as some have criticized. It certainly doesn't mean "take stupid risks pointlessly." Rather, it is a battle cry. Fear is not a stopping point, and shyness is not a permanent condition. I didn't become comfortable standing up in front of crowds overnight. I didn't push my boundaries in travel and adventure in a day. I'm not comfortable with public speaking, risk-taking, or extroversion because these are inborn traits.

I learned—or more accurately, I taught myself—to be bold through practice. If extroversion is about being outgoing, taking risks, and putting yourself out there, then it is a skill. Not a personality trait. Of course there are psychological predispositions in which we may or may not place stock, but to call ourselves by these titles is to do ourselves a disservice. It is to excuse ourselves from the challenge of ever pushing past our starting point. It is to bind our wrists with labels and our feet with subjective limitations.

I started out shy, quiet, cautious, but I won't end that way. There are only three steps to this process of stepping beyond our self-imposed limits. I practice them pretty much every day, and I owe a lot to this simple formula. It goes as follows:

1. Feel the fear.
2. Do it anyway.
3. Rinse, and repeat.

Shy? Quiet? Introverted? Cautious? I see you, and I see the vagabondess waiting to grow with you as you challenge these labels and explore the outer reaches of your personality.

Community (How to Find It Anywhere)

As you've probably realized, I drop myself into cities and countries where I know no one on a regular basis. And despite cultural and linguistic barriers, I find community there, wherever "there" is. The longer I travel, the more my community network looks like one of those light-up maps of the World Wide Web. Nodes in every continent, interconnecting lines of acquaintance, friendship, work, and family creating a high-tech pattern of human relationships made visible. And the older I get, the more I appreciate the role that community plays in my life; these solo quests wouldn't quite make sense without that futuristic backdrop of glowing connections. While finding community in a totally new place may seem somewhat inaccessible at first, it is truly just a practice like any other. Anyone can do it with the help of a few tools and techniques.

First, reach out to anyone who might be able to connect you with people in your new temporary home. A simple "Do I know anyone in _____?" on Facebook can yield unexpected results. This method has found me friends in otherwise totally anonymous destinations from Prague and Montenegro to Berlin, Sicily, and more. Asking, "Does anyone have any connections in _____?" has yielded equally helpful introductions to friends of friends. The more I travel, the more this network grows, seemingly exponentially. I hear that there are apps for this too, but I can't speak from experience. Apps like travelstoke and Travello advertise connecting you with locals willing to share information or other travelers looking for buddies.

Second, embrace your vulnerability. Ask questions, get lost, feel afraid. There is no need to read travel forums, or even look up directions (although by all means do both if it sets your mind at ease). The information you need is waiting for you on the ground. Ask for directions, ask for help, ask for a hug. It's scary to need something from someone, especially a stranger. Welcome to the world of solo travel! Vulnerability is not weakness; it is the closest we have to a magic spell for making friends and connecting to new communities.

> "Vulnerability is the birthplace of connection."
> —Brene Brown

Third, keep doing you. If you love permaculture, set up a work-trade through websites like WWOOF, Workaway, and NuMundo and join an intentional community that shares your values and lifestyle. If you love to surf, set your sights on a world-class surf destination and plug into a community of like-minded folks. Follow your passions. Being a vagabondess doesn't mean you can't do or be anything else. When I travel, I always carry two extra pairs of shoes with me: dance and climbing. Dancing tango in Kenya, salsa-ing in Berlin, and climbing in Cape Town, I've connected with people I never would have met otherwise. Same goes for surfing in Morocco and hiking in Spain. Do the things you love to do, and you'll find your people anywhere.

And finally, seek some kind of familiarity in the chaos. Ground into a new place by becoming a regular customer in a cafe, restaurant, or even corner store. Find comfort in simply being recognized by someone. When our default mode is anonymity, feeling seen, known, and familiar offers a powerful sense of place. Especially when I have a few weeks or months somewhere, I find myself accumulating these "regular" spots. Though utterly departing from all known routine is a key, even necessary element of travel for me, glimpses of familiarity within the unknown provide welcome, even necessary moments of respite. Places of worship, musical jams, or sports teams may also provide you with a sense of community and belonging while far away from the familiar. Whatever feels nourishing, connected, and meaningful, do that.

Lonely Time

2015, Sicily, Italy

I have just enough space in my Airbnb room to roll out my yoga mat. I follow online classes or do my own practice in the morning, then sit in my private kitchen (a godsend, given how emotional I've been getting while chopping onions) to do a few hours of editing work. Afternoons find me savoring almond or pistachio granita (similar to gelato, but icier) at a nearby cafe. I soak in the fragile peace of each moment and write pages of stream-of-consciousness nonsense. I go for long walks in this forgotten medieval town and keep conversations with strangers short and superficial. In the evenings, I give space to the tears that need to fall, prepare simple meals with local ingredients like ricotta, tomatoes, and olives, and write angsty poetry not meant to be shared.

It has been a difficult transition out of partnership. I suppose it usually is. I do not want to pretend everything is okay. I do not want to talk to strangers. I crave support and care from friends, but clearly I need to heal alone, because I have chosen to spend two weeks in a place where I know absolutely no one. This isn't quite solitude; there is a feeling of lack or absence. Something or someone missing. Yet, that shadowy absence holds me and supports me in a way that, perhaps, friends could not. I sink into it gratefully, and after two weeks, I feel more or less ready to step back into normal social interactions again.

———

When all else fails, fail. We can't be friendly and outgoing all of the time. That's okay. In fact, it's normal! Sometimes the challenge of the unknown shifts from exhilarating to tiresome for any number of reasons. When that happens, I take time to write, read, call friends and family, and simply be. This lifestyle of exploration and discovery has curves and cycles, just like any other. These moments of pause—you can call them solo travel fails, but I think of them as pauses—make the adventure all the richer.

I would define loneliness as times of unbidden solitude and silence. The days where we really, really want to have a conversation with someone, *anyone*, but no one on our twelve-hour bus ride is interested. The evenings where we're dying to snuggle with someone, but we're in a remote cabin in the mountains designed for extreme isolation. The sudden bursts of longing for *someone special to share it with* that punctuate our solo travel bliss. In these moments—solitude no longer a welcome balm, but rather a tiresome burden—we feel lonely.

Good. Just as openness does not make sense without closedness, abundance means nothing without emptiness, and blissful solitude has little value without melancholy loneliness to balance it. The shadow side of this lifestyle is lovely in the way that a stormy day is lovely. I invite you to look at it hard and long. Constant sungazing is bad for your eyes, and besides, a vagabondess' freedom has form and lightness only because of the shadows it casts.

There is really only one solution for the more challenging emotions that invariably arise in solo travel: *Allow them*. Loneliness, nostalgia, homesickness, insecurity, longing—they are all part of this whole "being a human with a vast array of emotions" thing. Open your eyes in the darkness. Look at your monsters directly. Learn their names. Say hello. And then move past them, stepping back into wild joyfulness. And then go back to the shadows, again. It is a cycle that, as far as I know, has no end. It is called being alive.

Solitude, sociability, silence, noise, loneliness, community. The vagabondess embraces all of it. Welcome to the journey.

> "The good life… cannot be mere indulgence. It must contain a measure of grit and truth."
> —Yi-Fu Tuan

IF I COULD FLY

What are you looking for?
I am searching…
I am searching for—
I am searching, because
it is only in movement that I find stillness.
In running I am free;
In dancing I am liberated.
But if I could fly—
Ah if I could fly,
I would be truly
Boundless.

V. Movement

Stillness, Slow Travel, & Eco-Consciousness

August, 2017, Vermont

It's 1:04 p.m., and the sun is hitting my laptop screen at just the right angle, forcing me to squint to see what I write. The bus rattles and sways on the two-lane Vermont highway. Pen and paper prove unusable. I have music in my ears, and it makes me think of caravan routes through the desert, the rolling gait of long-legged animals on sand, the scorching white heat of a cloudless sky at noon.

I look out the window to my left and witness another set of elements entirely—green mountains, gentle New England sky. Yet the felt sense is the same. It is a tenuous impression I have tried and failed to describe so many times, I nearly believe it is impossible to do so. It is the thing that calls me to move and whispers instructions to my intuition. It is the thing that taught me to dance, barefoot and alone. "Wanderlust" is an incomplete surrogate for the thing I mean.

I look outside again. There is a story in the sky, like always; I could spend the whole ride watching the shapeshift-

ing drama and chuckling to myself. Mountains undulate on the horizon, soft and green and melodic; I could spend the whole ride tapping out their rhythm against my thigh. Walls of trees enter and leave my sight, as varied yet indistinct as an ocean of faces in a crowded subway car. I could spend the whole ride absorbing their anonymous features. I could spend the whole ride sitting here doing nothing too—and for someone who loves to do things, that's already remarkable.

What is this thing that calls me to move and calms me through action? What is it about being in motion—in trains or on foot, by boat, or in dance—that soothes my mind into a stillness I have never found in sitting meditation? What is it about being in motion that, like an embodied lullaby, so entrances me—and I suspect so entrances many other lovers of movement?

The answer is in the question. Movement entrances. It occupies us—or at least it occupies me—so fully that there is absolutely no space for thoughts of elsewhere. Other times, other people, other places... these disappear in the all-pervading "this-ness" of moving. (Moving my body through space or being moved through space, it hardly matters, so long as the coordinates change fast enough to leave thoughts and worries behind.)

For many years now, I have been writing about the inner stillness that arises when all else is in flux. I experience this same outcome in yoga and ecstatic dance, aerial arts, and contact improv. I think it's safe to say that this magic stillness is my only addiction. A single taste will have you seeking it again for the rest of your life.

A vagabondess knows this. A dancer knows this. A meditator or yogi knows this. However you step outside the borders *of your skin and embrace the "this-ness" of pure movement, you will never be satisfied to remain inside the lines again.*

In my years of vagabonding, I have heard two things more often than anything else: "What are you looking for?" and, "I hope you find what you're looking for." But it's not a "what." It is a "how." It is a voice that calls me to move and a sense of boundlessness that keeps me coming back. It is a way of moving through life and through space. It is not a thing I can find and then be done with. It is the searching that gives meaning and form to the sought. And so we vagabondesses keep chasing shadows through the desert and melodies through the mountains. We keep seeking stillness in movement.

———

A SOLO JOURNEY IS A FASCINATING study of movement in all its forms: slowness, reckless speed, stillness, inertia, beginnings, endings, and middles. Exploring every facet of the phenomenon of movement—travel through physical and mental space—the vagabondess will learn as much about herself as she does about the world. What will I do with a thirty-hour ferry ride? How do I manage my carbon footprint? How do I know when it's time to leave? Even worse, how do I know when it's time to stay? Let's try to answer those questions.

Travel Slow (Literally)

It's 8:15 a.m. on the *Grandi Navi Veloci* ferry from Tangier, Morocco to Barcelona, Spain. I look up from my breakfast—a sad assortment of boxed orange juice, cold croissant and drinkable cappuccino—and observe the other diners. Some are in groups or pairs. Many are young Moroccan families. Many are alone.

Of this last group, few are doing anything (checking phones, or even reading). They're just sitting there, drinking coffee, looking around. It reminds me of Johnny Cash's famous response when asked for his definition of paradise: "This morning, with her, having coffee." I'm not even a particular Johnny Cash fan, but something about that phrase—or more, the slowness it implies—fits this mood.

People choose to travel by ferry (around thirty hours from Tangier to Barcelona, rather than two or three by plane) for many reasons. The slightly cheaper cost. The relative ease and comfort of sleeper cabins and lots of space to roam. The vaguely romantic allure of faded, Titanic-style old world luxury.

I suspect some people choose it for the slowness, too. Sitting in a deck chair for hours, watching the boat's trailing wake. Pacing the endless red-carpeted hallways, hands skimming smudged brass banisters, stepping inside and outside and inside again with no particular aim.

Sitting there, drinking coffee, looking around. Because there's nothing better to do. Because the boat will get there, slowly, and we have time. Because, just like Johnny Cash, we recognize that the smallest moments contain the whole universe—if we slow down enough to dwell there for a while.

For me, this is the essence of slow travel: dwelling in a moment while everything shifts around us, knowing that we're on our way. I prefer to travel by boat, train, or foot whenever possible. I dream of traveling by horseback; one day I will do so. If there is a longer, more scenic route, I probably want to take it. My ears perk up at the words, "or you could walk there…"

Slow travel, like slow food, implies dedication to the whole process. It's not only about the destination; it's not only about the finished meal on your plate. It is the journey—the quality of the soil, the taste of the water, the warmth of a stranger's gaze—that makes the destination so delicious. We can only experience those subtle details by slowing down, forfeiting our twenty-first-century inclination towards instant gratification, and finding the magic in a cup of coffee.

I've taken more absurdly long train, bus, and ferry rides than I could possibly count. Barcelona to London: Why go in two hours when you can take two days? Stockholm to Turku: Thirteen hours and no regrets! Goa to Kolkata: In hindsight, maybe forty hours was a bit long. I do realize that whiling away an entire day or more on a sluggish transport system can be a challenge at first. I haven't forgotten my astonishment at my fellow passengers in Nepal, where I took some of my first twelve-hour bus journeys in 2013. They put me to shame, doing nothing for the entire journey, never complaining, and maintaining perfect serenity during the hours of touch-and-go traffic leaving Kathmandu Valley.

So if you find the thought of a thirty-hour ferry ride daunting, or positively terrifying, here are a few suggestions on how to pass the time:

1. **People watch.** The man in the seat behind me telling another passenger how he never learned how to read words, only concepts. The woman across the aisle discussing, at length, a petty workplace drama. The endless procession of human faces, voices, expressions—mundane and extraordinary at once. It's better than Netflix!

2. **Make things.** Activities that occupy the hands but leave the mind free to wander are ideal for long trips. I love to crochet, make origami cranes, or play with macrame.

3. **Read.** Bring a fresh book you know you'll love. The longer the better. If you'd happily sit on the couch with a good book all day, your daytime hours are sorted.

4. **Write.** Whether or not you're a writer is beside the point. Write down observations, streams of consciousness, or the funny things people say while you're eavesdropping.

5. **Make lists.** If you can't think of anything else to write, there are always lists. I happen to love lists— the way they sit uselessly on my desktop after I make them, their satisfying list-ness, the irrational sense of efficiency I feel when writing them. They might even come in handy when you arrive at your destination.

6. **Eat.** On travel days, I drop any preferences or pretenses I usually have about food. Cherries and leftovers. Chocolate and chips. While normally I wouldn't advocate for eating out of boredom, long rides are a special exception. Entering a liminal

space, free from the normal constraints of time and metabolic physics, is one of the advantages of traveling this way, after all.

7. **Work.** Just kidding—travel days aren't work days! Be it a lack of reliable wifi or the soporific rattling of tracks, these journeys don't usually support much work. But if you really need to get things done, there's certainly plenty of time.

8. **Do nothing.** Nothing, nothing, nothing. Stare out the window and daydream about mountains that hold up the sky. Close your eyes and turn the rattle of the train into music. Lean back, put your hands in your lap, and just sit there. I think we could all do with a little more nothing these days. A ten-hour train or thirty-hour ferry ride is a good place to start.

9. **Anything else.** Listening to music, meditating, talking to strangers, walking up and down the aisles, stretching, deleting old files off your phone, breathing—there is so much to do, you may not even have time for it all!

And what about walking? Since walking the Camino de Santiago, a month-long journey across Northern Spain, I've been particularly enamored of the most ancient of all transport systems: two lovely feet. If you've never done any long-distance walking, you may be wondering, *What is it even like to spend your whole day walking? Don't you get bored?*

Well, let me tell you.

June 2016, Camino de Santiago

What is it like to do nothing but walk? Time-consuming, for starters. I've barely had time to read or write, let alone eat or sleep. And yet, it's not boring, and it's not monotonous. Of course, at the end of these long days I have been tired and anxious to arrive, but I have not regretted the hours spent walking. The landscape always lush and changing. The weather always a blessing—or a curse—and a mystery. The body always master, limited by thirst, hunger, and inflamed muscles. The details always important. And always, always the yellow painted arrows pointing the way... no, it's not boring. It leaves little space for that which lies outside of walking. To check emails and work for an hour is terribly jarring. Mind full of sky and trees and aching feet, and it is enough. It is enough.

I've talked with enough fellow pilgrims by now to mark a Camino phenomenon: Few Deep Thoughts. As one woman put it, "I'm mostly just wondering how far the next town is, or thinking about how my legs hurt." Or as another said, "If I think anything it's, 'Oh, that's pretty.'"

The same goes for me. I probably say, "Wow, that's gorgeous," or "Look how beautiful that is" several dozen times a day. If I do have deep thoughts, they are few and buried in layers of baseline chatter. I am far, far more likely to think about nothing at all.

Similar to Few Deep Thoughts, another common thread I've noticed: No Transformative Moments. The sky hasn't opened, except to rain. I haven't had any epiphanies about myself or the world. The days and weeks have been terribly steady, plodding on with a rhythm strikingly reminiscent of footsteps. Pretty much the opposite of a series of life-changing moments.

If transformation is happening, it is very subtle, much like the imperceptibly changing landscape, architecture, people. We don't notice it shifting until we've passed by, but then—but then!—the difference is so very obvious.

If the idea of spending days, weeks, or even months in the frame of mind described above is appealing to you, I highly encourage you to give it a try.

Conscious Vagabonding

It is critical to mention mindful or conscious travel at some point in this book. As slow travel happens to be one of the best ways to lighten our carbon footprint, this seems like the right place for it.

Global air travel continues to rise rapidly even as warnings about climate change become ever more urgent, with planes carrying over four billion passengers every year. In 2018, aviation accounted for 2% of global, human-produced carbon dioxide emissions. This number is also expected to rise by around 700% by 2050. These emissions are directly responsible for disasters like melting ice caps, rising sea levels, pollution, and global warming. We already know all this, but many air travelers pretend we don't know, or that it has nothing to do with us. I believe that we travelers have a responsibility to at least consider the impact of our restlessness. What we do with those considerations is up to each of us.

Regardless of the choices we make (limiting air travel,

boycotting it completely, or deciding to proceed with our usual habits, for instance), I believe that slow travel can bring meaningful shifts to our own perspective and to our carbon footprint. This mode of travel opens space and time not just for deeper enjoyment and appreciation of a place, but also for deeper reflection on our impact there.

And lest anyone tell you otherwise, you do not have to travel to the other side of the world to be a vagabondess. Remember: vagabonding is a state of mind. You can experience rich and transformative journeys to the next town over, to the woods behind your house, or to the wilderness in your own mind. Keeping your carbon footprint small will be far less complicated, and you will still discover unique adventures into yet-uncharted territories of your own life. I do not feel I can preach this approach, as it is not the way I chose to travel for many of my vagabondess years to date, but I do wish to mention this alternative.

Mindful travel is about more than our carbon footprint. I would sum it up like this: For a journey to be mindful, the vagabondess must bring awareness to the impact of her travels on the environment, on local communities and economies, and on herself. More than anything, being a conscious traveler requires us to ask a lot of questions:

About our mode of transport: Is there a more environmentally friendly way to get there? If not, can I offset my carbon emissions by donating to an organization that directly works to sequester carbon back into the earth? (FlyGRN is a great resource for this.) Should I stay three months in one place, rather than trying to hit every country in Europe as quickly as possible? How about staying a year?

About our money: Where are my tourist dollars going when I buy this souvenir—to a factory halfway across the world, or to a nearby women's cooperative? Am I supporting small local initiatives or big foreign corporations by staying at this hotel or hostel? Is there a way to shift my behavior so that more of my money stays in the hands of the people truly earning it?

About our consumption: Is there an alternative to this plastic packaging? Do I really need this thing I'm about to buy? Were these materials sustainably sourced? Where and how were the ingredients for my breakfast produced? What industries does my purchase support? Are they extractive or regenerative?

About the politics of representation: Who holds power in this society? Is my tour guide, cab driver, or Airbnb host representing only the experience of the dominant group, or are they offering a more nuanced perspective? Who else can I talk to in order to understand the complex array of identities inhabiting this place? Who is running this museum, tour, or experience? In what ways might that influence the stories they tell?

About ourselves: Who do I want to be? How do I want to interact with this new culture, new person, new environment? What fears are stopping me from truly opening to all this newness? How can I grow as an individual through this journey? How might my conditioned assumptions and expectations color everything about my experience?

And finally, about our own set of values: Do I care? In this moment, do I want this Starbucks latte more than I want to support local enterprise? In this moment, do I want to go to Costa Rica to visit Toby more than I want to avoid air travel? In this moment, do I just want to lie on the beach and not think about plastic waste, women's rights, or climate change? Where am I willing to compromise? Where are the hard lines in my personal ethics?

Only you can answer those last sets of questions. Already in the asking, you are on your way to a more conscious approach to moving through the world.

> "A journey makes such a particular shape [...] Perhaps it is because all the experience is rooted in you, the choice and manner of the journey must be yours."—Jennifer Lash

Staying

Another simple way to reduce our carbon footprint is to "travel" less—in the sense of moving through space with tons of emissions—by staying longer wherever we go. Again, work-trades are an excellent option for staying longer at little to no cost. So are location-independent work positions that allow you to set up shop wherever you choose to put down temporary roots. In all fairness, I was not always an advocate for staying a while. In 2013, I passed through about twenty countries in less than a year. In the heyday of my hitchhiking phase, I would sometimes stay just a night or two in one country before hopping over the border to the next one. (It's easier to do in Europe, where those borders are very close together.)

And if that kind of perpetual movement is calling to you, by all means, live that adventure.

However, if you vagabond long enough, you will likely feel called to slow down and stay a bit longer one of these days. Don't panic. You'll know when that time has come. It comes back to intuition—the soft voice that speaks from our gut and pretty much always has the right answer if we practice hearing it. When that voice speaks, urging us to *stay, stay awhile, this is a good place to rest your feet*, we would do well to listen to it. You can always come up with a dozen rational explanations to offer to your friends and family about why you will be spending the next four months in Kenya or the next year in Costa Rica. But you'll know that, really, the reason is far simpler and far less rational: *It just feels right.*

"There is a voice that doesn't use words, listen."
—Rumi

I have been based in Costa Rica for nearly three years now. It is the longest I have stayed in one place since leaving Vermont in 2014. It has been a baffling process for this vagabondess to decode, but one rich in its own lessons and growth edges. While it is difficult to relinquish, even briefly, the taste of perpetual movement, there are also many sweet advantages to sticking around: Getting to know—and be known in—a local community on a deeper level. Achieving fluency in a new language. Focusing all the energy of travel into other kinds of creative projects, relationships, or inner work. Finally being able to return the generosity of so many wonderful friends and couchsurfing hosts from all over the world. Staying has a very different flavor indeed, but equally rich.

A word of warning. As an expat or foreigner who won't leave, you should get used to two constant questions: "Where are you from?" and, "Why are you here?" As a vagabondess, you will likely come to understand that these questions entirely miss the point.

"Where are you from?" assumes that our home is somewhere else. In reality, home is something we carry with us—a few musty belongings stuffed into a backpack, and an unshakeable sense of belonging in our own skin. Home is a smell, like sage burning or garlic frying. Home is a melody, your favorite song blasting in the kitchen. Home is a feeling—belly relaxing and a grateful sigh of arriving. It is the absolute conviction that you exist wherever you are. Home is the soft skin and hard bones of your body—as transient and lovely as hardwood floors, red brick walls or picket fences. Home is sinking down into a comfortable chair (any chair). Home is a key turning in a lock (any key, and any lock). Home is not a "somewhere else" we must return to in order to feel complete.

"Home is where our heart sings."—Unknown

"Why are you here" assumes consistently rational decision-making. In reality, there is likely no straightforward "why" to explain our presence in this place. There may be little to no logic behind our decision to make our home here, rather than any other place. *Why are we here?* We will know the answer to that one only in hindsight, looking back on our path and exclaiming, "Ah, now I see."

Do not feel obliged to invent answers. It is okay to shrug your shoulders, lift up your hands and say, "I'll tell you when I find out!" It's also perfectly fine to dive into the long answer if you truly want to. Regardless of how you choose to respond, be prepared for these questions, for they are impossible to avoid.

Leaving

A backpack leans against the wall. The kitchen is clean. The lights, off. Curtains, drawn. You look around one last time, step into the hallway, and shut the door. You walk to the bus, metro, or train station and take the next ride to the airport. You sit down and close your eyes, but you don't sleep. Instead, you run your thoughts over the past days, weeks, months, or perhaps years—the people you've met, the food you've cooked, the dances you've danced.

It is a ritual of sorts, this taking stock. There is so much to remember, and you want to pay each face, each meal, each moment the homage it deserves. Of course, you can't really remember it all, but you do what you can and take time for reflection. Perhaps you allow a sweet sigh of nostalgia, but you do not second guess your decision. It is time to leave.

Just as you will know when the time has come to stay for a while, you will also know when it is time to pack your bags once again and return to the road.

The above scenario describes hundreds of departure days in my personal history. As a vagabondess, I have become an expert in goodbyes. I can pack my bag in ten minutes tops, and I know exactly how much time to leave to avoid unnecessary stress at train stations or airports. The logistics of leaving are a science, and I have studied well. However, after so many years on the road, I know one thing for certain: It doesn't get easier. Not for me.

I think a lot of people have an image in their head of the free-spirited nomad-hippie who wanders the world without attachments and lets go of people and places easily. And those people certainly exist. I know a few of them! For many travelers like myself, however, the non-attachment is an illusion, a misperception, or both. From our perspective, leave-taking is the difficult-yet-necessary counterpoint to arriving. *If I don't leave, I can never arrive.* So I do leave. But it is never easy.

The more deeply we connect with the people and places we visit, the harder it gets. That's one of the consequences of slow travel. Slow travel isn't just about how we get there; it's about how we stay. For me, that has meant getting deep wherever I go. Of course, success in this endeavor has its consequences. I have been continually falling in love with cities, mountains, people, dogs, and cafes for so many years. This love, wonder, passion—call it what you will—makes my experiences what they are, but it also makes leaving that much more complicated. Yet I have still left, more times than I can count. I pack my bag(s), look around one last time, step outside, and shut the door.

There is a heaviness to this repeated ritual of leaving, perhaps difficult to understand if you do not live in movement. And if movement is not your creed, you may wonder, *If it's not easy or carefree, why do you do it?* I suppose it comes back, again, to intuition. Sometimes, it is simply time to leave.

A vagabondess does not leave without sadness or nostalgia. She does not leave without a care, hair blowing in the ocean breeze and sunlight casting long shadows on the path behind her. But when the wind of intuition pushes her toward the door, she does leave. Three certainties have softened many a difficult departure, and perhaps can do the same for you. I believe the following to be true:

1. It is in fact always possible to go back, to revisit, to return to a place.
2. Goodbyes are part of a balanced life. If we don't leave, we cannot arrive.
3. Heaviness is as vital as lightness; one who wishes to live in movement must understand both.

Coming Back "Home"

> "And once the storm is over, you won't remember how you made it through, how you managed to survive. You won't even be sure whether the storm is really over. But one thing is certain. When you come out of the storm, you won't be the same person who walked in."—Haruki Murakami

And when we return (if we return, that is)? This is quite possibly the hardest part of the journey. We all know this. It's archetypal stuff: The Hero's Journey. Step One, answer the call to adventure. Step Two, face obstacles. Step

Three, return home victorious. Of all the obstacles, it is the return home that proves most treacherous for our hero or heroine. Remember how Odysseus' epic journey ends?

So, we vagabond. We heed the call to adventure. We gather so much beauty, so much wisdom, so much knowing. We face our obstacles, the treacherous wilderness beyond the limits of our known world, and we are ready for a victorious return. But how *do* we bring those lessons home—into the body, into the mind, into the world? The heart-opening, horizon-shattering, mind-expanding experience of a solo journey is the first step, not the end of the road. For every obstacle we overcome, there is a higher one around the bend. For every road we walk, there is a longer one still to travel. For every difficult journey we complete, there are yet more turbulent waters to navigate up ahead.

The return. Everything that follows. We inevitably come back from our journeys changed. More sombre, or more joyful. Heavy with nostalgia, or lighter with all the baggage we have dropped along the way. Wiser, or more innocent—or both. In a few months or years, we live more lifetimes than we could hope. We die small deaths, traverse dark nights, and emerge at dawn with new perspective. And in the wake of this transformation and growth, we quite possibly return home. Back to people who love us, yet perhaps cannot understand the new layers of self that we have unearthed. Back to places that feel familiar, yet inaccessible.

Don't worry. A vagabondess is a chameleon. She can slip in and out of the garments of her old life, even when they don't quite fit anymore. She can still follow the old rules of time, of dress, of conduct. She can even still enjoy it, genuinely connecting with the characters and trappings that surround her past self. However, she will not be the same as she was before. She will never be the same. She has traveled far. She has met dragons. She has shed the layers of herself, and now she puts them back on, although they fit different, feel different, look different.

A vagabondess invariably returns full of questions. She has said hello to the unknown and moved beyond it. She has touched secrets and tasted their blessings on her tongue, her skin, her heart. There is no turning back, dear vagabondess, but don't worry. You'll find everything else exactly as you left it, or nearly so.

ODE TO A POWERFUL WOMAN

You came into this world dancing—
Dancing to earth-beat,
moon-beat,
heartbeat.

Your feet did not
whisper apologies,
but stomped
defiantly
a message of strength:

"I am here,"
your body declared,
"And I will take up
no less space
than what I am."

You
are a powerful woman.
You set fire
to convention
and bury limitations
beneath the fertile soil
of your soul;

You flood
their expectations
in the fury
of your blood,

and scatter
their pretensions
with mocking laughter
in your voice.

You
are a powerful woman.

You bow to no one
but the earth
and the moon
and the wisdom of trees.

You reside
in your heart,
in your body,
in your power in your heart;
in your power,
you abide…

You
are a powerful woman.

Your toes
are roots,
stubborn.

Your voice
is thunder,
bold.

Your heart
is soil,
life-giving.

Your sweat
is ocean,
healing.

Your life
is earth-beat,
moon-beat,
wing-beat—

Sweet
uncompromising
presence
in power—
in presence
in power, in power, in power.

You,
friend, sister, goddess,
are a powerful woman,
and we are
so glad
you're here.

VI. Health

My Body is Well

I WILL NEVER FORGET THE STORY a dear vagabond friend shared with me and a group of intrepid students as we crossed the Greek island of Samothraki on foot. Between wilderness skills training, walking eight hours per day, and cooking rice and pasta over an open fire, we found time for stories too. The harsh mountain landscape and crackling campfires invited intimate listening and an ancient sense of kinship, rapidly knit.

This tale in particular touched the group, inspiring us to sing in the most challenging moments of our trek. It is the story of a West African musician named Olotunje who moves to New York City. Every morning, he wakes up at dawn, walks out onto the balcony of his apartment, stretches out his arms, and sings at the top of his lungs, "*ARRAMILÈ, ARRAMILÈ.*"

At first, his neighbors complain and shout at him to be quiet, but he keeps going out there every morning to stretch and sing. Eventually the neighbors give up, and they join in instead. "If you can't beat 'em..." Olotunje's tenacity shows us how one voice has the power to transform an entire community—or an entire New York City apartment block.

"Arramilè" translates as, "My body is well."

I love this story and have proceeded to share it with many of my groups for retreats or workshops. It brings me back to that arduous trek through the mountains of Samothraki, and it recalls the sense of community I felt amongst our band of wanderers. Perhaps most importantly, it reminds me of the confidence in and gratitude for my body that a few syllables can invoke. I find three main lessons in Olotunje's story, which can be of great benefit to a vagabondess:

1. Persistent good cheer can wear down just about any negativity directed our way.
2. Wellness is (often) a state of mind.
3. Health is just as contagious as illness.

Traveling solo, we are likely to encounter minor—and major—health bumps along the road. Traveler's diarrhea is nearly inevitable, especially if you want to try all the street food (I certainly do!). Colds and flus wreak havoc on hostels, communities, and other shared living situations. Accidents happen; scrapes and bangs are as common in travel as they are back home.

It can be scary to deal with these things far from the comforts of our own bed, language, and familiar medicines. There is absolutely nothing enjoyable about recovering from illness or injury without the support of family or close friends. However, those three lessons are a strong foundation for staying healthy as much as possible.

"Don't You Fuck With My Energy"

A scene from a short stay in northern Thailand in 2013 floats to the surface of my memory: Two tuk-tuks stopped on the side of a dirt road at around eleven p.m. Four righteous backpackers and a very angry tuk-tuk driver illuminated by the flashing lights at the remote party kicking into gear just behind them. The backpackers are arguing over the previously-agreed-upon fare. The difference works out to just a few cents each. The driver is near-hysterical.

My new acquaintances and soon-to-be ex-travel companions eventually pay up, our drivers zip off in a huff, and we enter the party in a deluge of negativity and indignant complaints. I had tentatively planned to travel onward with these "new friends," but their behavior has left me feeling extremely uncomfortable, and I adjust my plans to allow our paths to diverge. I do not need that kind of negativity—and terrible tourist manners—in my journey.

If you've never heard the song *Bruja* by Princess Nokia, go ahead and give it a listen. The bridge is unavoidably catchy: "Don't you fuck with my energy," she repeats over and over and over again. It has become one of my favorite travel slogans. Good health is about much more than our physical body. Energetic health, in short, depends on what we allow in, and what we keep at a distance. Let me break that down.

If we're traveling solo and link up with a group of travelers who are constantly complaining—about the rain, the food, the accommodations, the cost of *every-*

thing—that negativity is going to rub off on us. (Case in point: the scene in Thailand described above.) By choosing to continue traveling in that atmosphere of dissatisfaction, we are allowing that energy into our sphere of orbit. To create distance, we may choose to stay longer in a place and let our companions move ahead. Or we may continue to travel with them for any number of reasons but take more time for solo adventures, refuse to play the game when the complaining starts, and seek out other people who surf another, more upbeat wave.

Another perilous route to bad travel energy is FOMO: Fear Of Missing Out. It's an insidious thought pattern and wildly contagious in this age of social media and incessant sharing (bragging). If left untreated, this condition can take over a person's thoughts, souring every adventure with the creeping doubt that it could have been even better. The best alternative to FOMO I have seen thus far is JOMO—the Joy Of Missing Out. Take pleasure in what you are doing (or not doing) rather than give your time and energy to feeling envy toward other people's experiences. This goes for the vagabondess-to-be, too. It's not about what you're missing; it's about where you are now. Bring joy and adventure to the lifestyle you have. You can try on another for size whenever you are ready. Listen to other travelers' stories with curiosity, of course, as there is much to learn from their failures and successes, but beware of fear or self-doubt slinking in with visions of distant, inaccessible marvels. Their travel joy does not invalidate your own. Every journey is its own. Every vagabondess is on her path, and it could not be otherwise.

More than anyone else, though, it is often friends or family at home who are most prone to "fuck with our energy." Envy, doubt, fear, and pessimism deeply affect our journey, even at a distance. When loved ones end phone calls with a dubious "Well, I hope you're happy," that scepticism can slip under our skin. When the words, "I hope you find what you're looking for" take on a passive aggressive edge, over time they can wear down our confidence in our choices. However, we have the power to transform this discourse. When the tone shifts in conversations with loved ones, we can flip the script, asking about their lives, insisting that, "Yes, we are happy, now let's talk about something else," and refusing to take the bait when things veer into the realm of pessimism.

To promote good energetic health, we can adopt simple practices that keep our focus on the beauty of our present moment experience:

- Taking time to feel and express gratitude for the life and experiences we have literally changes our neural patterning for the better.
- Sharing smiles, laughter, or hugs with people who make us feel good lifts us up physiologically, psychologically, and energetically.
- Seeking support from friends and loved ones who cheer on our growth paves our path of evolution, rather than setting up roadblocks.

(Of course, no one is upbeat all the time. We must also accept and even embrace other kinds of energy when they arise, so long as we don't get stuck there.)

Wellness Is a State of Mind

I love the story of "Arramilè" most of all for the awareness it brings to a basic truth: Wellness begins in the mind. "My body is well" is an affirmation, a belief, a statement. It carries no tangible weight; after all, these are only words. And yet, words can bring both healing and illness. As a vagabondess, you have a choice. You can choose to move through the world with fear—of bad people, bad luck, bad bacteria, bad health. Or you can choose to move through the world with confidence and trust—in people, in the universe, and in your own well-being. This should sound familiar; we've already talked about it in Chapter 3. You can choose to affirm your health. Or you can worry yourself into sickness. (I'm not saying our thoughts are solely responsible for our health and well-being. Bad luck strikes, bad bacteria really do exist, and shit happens. However, I do believe that we can cultivate a *predisposition* for health that begins in our own mental patterns.)

Bacteria, infections, and contagious diseases are all very real. In the section below, I will discuss some practical measures you can take to stay healthy as you journey. However, I genuinely believe that our mindset is a major determinant of good or bad health. Take food, for example. Travelers often worry obsessively about the cleanliness of the food on their plates. I've had my fair share of stomach bugs, and they really are *the worst*. In fact, I suspect I may still have a sneaky parasite hanging out in my gut, biding its time. Still, when I eat food at a remote bus stop, accept a meal or cup of tea in someone's home, or bite into a piece of fruit fresh from the market without washing it off first, I'm not thinking about bacteria. I'm thinking about the exquisite flavor of a juicy mango, the indulgent crunch of something fried and too salty, or the extraordinary kindness of a family I've only just met sharing their evening meal with me. To put it simply, I focus on what's right about this food, not about what could go wrong.

Furthermore, if our thought patterns are unhealthy—constantly judging others, criticizing ourselves, indulging in spiteful FOMO, or obsessively worrying about the worst case scenario—these patterns, too, trickle down into our bodies. We all know what judgment, fear, stress, or spite feel like in our body: a tensing of the stomach; a clenching of the heart or throat; a shortening of the breath; a tightening behind the eyes. Pay attention the next time your thoughts take you in this direction, and observe the physical effects. They will be there. Over time, this tension has real consequences for our physical health. Maintain your well-being by watching your thoughts and transforming negative thought patterns into healthier ones: from judgment to celebration of others' successes, from self-flagellation to self-love and affirmation, and from anxiety and criticism to calm, love, and gratitude. I believe there are entire books dedicated to this process, should you wish to find further instruction.

In a nutshell, though, what does it look like in practice to cultivate a mindset of wellness? There are libraries of information on this, but to start, take a page from Olotunje's book. You don't have to shout from your balcony (although you could!), but consider beginning your day with grateful affirmation of what you have: a body capable of carrying you along this vagabondish journey. Breath that nourishes your cells with new oxygen at a staggering rate. A mind capable of taking in so much new information, every moment, and turning it into meaning. This is already more than enough; this is abundance.

"My body is well. I am alive." Bring this thought into each day with you. You may still pick up a few pesky travel bugs along the way, but your mental foundations will be much better equipped to bring you back into a healthy equilibrium.

Surround Yourself with Health

If being healthy is a priority, you can choose your destinations based on the lifestyle, climate, food, and culture in which you know you will thrive. For instance, if you always get sick in the winter, choose tropical climates. If your body loves the Mediterranean diet, head to Greece! If an easygoing, slow pace of life makes you feel happy and relaxed, immerse yourself in cultures that know how to slow things down and enjoy the simple pleasures.

After three years of Vermont winters, I vowed that I would never live in a cold winter climate again. Perhaps "never" was a bit strong, but I have kept that promise for the past six years. Despite being born and raised in chilly Boston, Massachusetts, I have come to realize that my body truly was made for the tropics. I thrive in hot weather, rarely get sick when the sun is shining, and could happily live on papaya and coconut for an indefinite amount of time. It is easy to be healthy when we travel to places that are abundant in fruit, vegetables, sun, and clean water. (We may of course choose destinations for other reasons, but we do so knowing that we may have to work harder to maintain our health.)

Now, living in Costa Rica, I appreciate the benefits of a healthy cultural climate even more than those of a meteorological one. "Pura vida" is a catchy tourist slogan, but it is also a fair summary of the lifestyle here. Translated literally to "pure life," it can be used as a greeting, to say goodbye, thank you, and you're welcome, or to answer the question, "How are you?" This multipurpose phrase encapsulates some of the warmth, community, and relaxed lifestyle I have found here. While not everything is as "pura vida" as the tourist brochures and tour guides might have you believe (story for another time), I have generally observed that Costa Ricans value family and community highly while taking a no-worries approach to obstacles like bad traffic, tropical storms, or bureaucratic delays.

I believe that health, optimism, and happiness are contagious. Just like Olotunje's neighbors, we can immerse ourselves in cultures of health and internalize the well-being of the people surrounding us.

Some Practical Things: Self-Care for Vagabondesses

Sure, okay, yes, there are also a few practical things that have nothing to do with energy or mental patterns that also help us to maintain good health, hygiene, and wellness while we travel. I recommend the following:

- **Drink clean water.** It is easier and easier to find filtered, safe drinking water even when you're far off the grid. Make sure your drinking water and even teeth-brushing water is purified, and you'll avoid most water-borne illnesses. There are great portable UV filters on the market too, which you can use to purify one liter of water at a time. Boiling water for several minutes is another option if there's no filtered water in sight. Avoid single-use plastic bottles, of course.

- **Eat clean food.** Depending on where you go, it may be incredibly easy or incredibly difficult to find local, organic food. Staying at ecovillages and communities is one way to ensure high food quality. In cities, if you're buying food at local markets, you can make your own choices about how and what you eat. Everything in moderation, of course; don't ever pass up an opportunity to enjoy a homemade meal, and don't even think about asking whether or not your generous hosts buy organic!

- **Cook.** Cooking has been the single most useful tool in my traveler's toolkit for staying healthy and grounded while on the road. Preparing at least some of my own meals, I get to control how I eat (mostly fruits, veggies, and whole grains) and how I source my ingredients (local markets whenever possible). Even more importantly, however, I get to connect with the place I am in through touch, smell, and taste as I buy and prepare those ingredients. This sense of connection to place is incredibly grounding and nourishing.

- **Walk everywhere.** Even if I don't specifically "exercise" for days, weeks, or months, I can easily stay reasonably active by walking everywhere, and my body thanks me for it. Plus, walking is a great way to really get to know a new place; I highly recommend it to you.

- **Go dancing.** My favorite way to get exercise, boost endorphins, and connect with local communities. This hits all the wellness goals at once! Don't love dancing? Find your ideal version of this, be it hitting up the local gym, signing up for an exercise class, joining a hiking group, or anything else that makes you feel excited to move your body and connect with new people at the same time.

- **Take care with substances.** Alcohol, tobacco, and other substances (drugs and sugar both fall into this category, in my book) are hard on both your health and your wallet. We all choose our own risks, and you are welcome to choose these substances as your health risk as I choose hitchhiking and acrobatics for mine. However, I suggest careful moderation when indulging in any addictive or toxic substances if you wish to optimize your health (and make the most of your budget) while on the road.

- **Develop a mindfulness practice.** Yoga, meditation, or anything else that encourages body awareness, presence, and calm will support you in moments of stress, keep your body healthy, and create space in your daily routine for introspection and grounded presence. Nowadays there are so many apps and websites for meditation or yoga, plus every hostel and intentional community usually has a packed schedule of wellness offerings, so it shouldn't be too difficult to integrate one of these practices into your journey.

- **Care for your sexual health.** Use protection. Have frank conversations with any sexual partners about their health status and relationship agreements. Clear communication is key; these conversations cannot be taboo. If you are at all sexually active, regardless of how careful you are, best practice is to get tested once or twice a year. De-stigmatize smart sexual health practices! Take control of your health!

- **Cherish sleep.** There will be nights that you don't sleep at all because you're sitting upright on an over-air conditioned bus, or nights you can't sleep because you're too excited about your journey to your next destination the following morning. However, I recommend getting into the habit of prioritizing sleep whenever you can. Just about any situation is easier to handle when you're well-rested.

- **Tune in.** Your body, mind, and heart know what they need to feel balanced, well, healthy, and happy. Take those cues. Give yourself the sleep, food, hydration, exercise, and stillness that you need. No one else knows exactly what that looks like; with practice, however, you'll develop a clearer and clearer sense of your own needs. Then, it's just a question of making it a priority to satisfy them.

Many people worry about staying healthy while traveling. Few consider the health benefits. Living a life free from routine challenges the brain and promotes neuroplasticity. Embracing change and unpredictability sharpens our ability to manage stress and stay calm in most situations. Constantly trying new things, tasting new foods, learning new languages, and meeting new people makes us resilient and adaptable. Exposing ourselves to new pathogens, tastes, smells, sights, and perspectives both strengthens our immune system and broadens our mental horizons.

Finally, a vagabondess learns that the act of wandering itself is uniquely healing. In embracing the solitude, freedom, challenges, and blessings of the open road, she discovers wellness in body, mind, heart, and spirit.

TO LOVE A GIRL WHO WANDERS

To love a girl who wanders, you must know that her soul yearns for movement.

The beat of a drum, the whistle of a train and the summit of a mountain are all the same language to her, urging her to move.

Your voice and your touch, too, can speak the language of movement. That is the second thing you must know. If a girl who wanders loves you, her soul will sway to the cadence of your words.

A girl who wanders sees poetry in everything, from the magnificence of the stars to the dance of a blade of grass.

If you love her, you must realize that you are poetry as well. Write her haikus in kisses and limericks in tiny gestures.

She will understand what you mean.

If you love a girl who wanders, run beside her. Not ahead of her or behind her, for both of these will quickly try her patience, but beside her. Do not follow or lead her to the highest peak or the tastiest food truck in sight; rather, join your paths and walk with her. Match your stride to hers, and she just might do the same.

This is a girl, a woman, a being who is accustomed to following her instincts and making her own way. She probably travels alone, makes friends easily on the road (bidding them farewell just as easily), and ignores the "Do Not Enter" sign.

Compromise does not come naturally to her. Be patient. The constant give and take of a relationship will take time for her to learn, but when she does, you will find her more generous, more compassionate than you could have imagined. For a girl who wanders has made a study of empathy.

She is made of water. She knows fluidity and change.

If you love a girl like this, you must discover the secret of holding her in your eyelashes, for she will slip through your fingers.

Sometimes the water in her will spill over. You don't have to ask why. Your presence is enough.

To love a girl who wanders, realize that wanderlust is a true affliction.

When her gaze is unfocused and her thoughts far away, know that she dreams not of other people, but of other worlds. Dream with her of caravans in the desert and sea journeys centuries ago. Help her plan road trips, buy plane tickets, or even build a tent in the living room when there are no better options.

Her craving for adventure cannot be suppressed for too long, and if you love a girl who wanders, you will be on the seat beside her when it is time to go.

To show this girl your love, bring her wildflowers and found objects—she will appreciate the journey that went into their gathering. Dance with her whenever you can. Share her joy as she spins, skirts flying outward. Listen to her stories, for she will have many—both true and remembered—and save your own in a carved hollow in your mind for when she asks you to tell her one.

To love a girl who wanders, be prepared to say yes.

Yes to adventures. Yes to treasure hunts and hopeless quests. Yes to a lifetime of searching. Do this, and she will, quite possibly, say yes to you.

A girl who wanders may not have many roots. You must offer her the depths of your heart and soul in which to plant sturdier ones. To act as soil and sustenance for another person's spirit is both a privilege and a responsibility—never take it lightly.

If you love a girl who wanders, only give her what she can carry—nothing bigger than your heart. Anything larger would be a waste. Accept her need to seek—strive to comprehend it, even—and comfort her when the leaves fall across her path and she feels lost.

Let her wander through the labyrinth of your mind, and marvel at the beauty she finds there. Hold her in your eyelashes, the lines of your hands and the ridges of your forehead, and wander with her.

VII. Love

Of Pirates & Vagabonds

"And still, after all this time,
The sun never says to the earth,
'You owe Me.'

Look what happens with
A love like that,
It lights the Whole Sky."

—Hafiz

LOVE ON THE ROAD. I could write a whole book about it. Maybe one day I will. It's hard to know where to begin... and where to stop. What is there to say, really, that could prepare you for it? We are never truly ready to fall in love, nor are we ever ready to lose it. As a vagabondess, you will likely do both, on repeat, for a long time.

I nearly didn't write this chapter. There are no rules or guidelines—a vagabondess roams through uncharted territory—so what can I possibly say that will be of use to you on your journey? My stories are hardly much help, and most are still too tender. Still, it feels important to write about this subject. It is one of the things women most often ask me about, worry about, and take as an excuse to ignore the call to ramble. Love and relationships are a fundamental, perhaps the fundamental element of human life, and this does not change just because we give up a fixed address. And finally, as a vagabondess who lives and travels with her heart wide open, I do believe I have gathered a few meaningful insights, which I would like to share with you.

To begin with, there is no one recipe for successful vagabond relationships. I know of many solo travelers who have stable, committed relationships back home. I know of many solo travelers who never have stable relationships with anyone. I know solo travelers who are promiscuous, and others who rarely connect intimately or romantically. Some hold traditional relationship values, while others practice various forms of non-monogamy. Obviously, there is no right answer, only many varied and valuable paths to human connection and fulfillment.

There was a time when I wrote often about love and romance. Poetry, essays, and lyrical odes to an idealized vision of the life of a vagabondess. That time has passed, or paused. The reality, after many years of nomadism, has proven far more challenging, and often less romantic, than I initially wanted to believe. It is not at all easy to love someone who walks the road less traveled—much harder to follow her, and even more difficult to keep up. Nor is it easy to return love in equal measure when one's heart is divided between a romantic partner and the entire world.

What's more, there is something inherently selfish about choosing this lifestyle, which perhaps in its very essence does not mesh well with conventional relationship models. To choose a partner and then match your path to theirs requires extensive compromise and commitment. A vagabondess, by nature, may find it difficult to compromise and commit. It's not impossible, of course, just difficult.

I have been called selfish many times for putting my dreams and my lifestyle first. Yet if it is selfish to be deeply in love with and committed to one's life path, then I'm okay with that label. The only life-long relationship we will ever have is with our own consciousness (and with the Universe, which I am inclined to think is the same thing). We owe it our fullest attention and love. It is important to remember this in moments of doubt or heartache. In choosing this path, we prioritize our own growth and dreams—always. Sometimes (romantic) love fits into that journey; sometimes it doesn't, and that's okay too.

A vagabondess always carries a deep well of love in her heart. Sometimes she shares it with others, and sometimes she shares it with herself.

Pirates & Vagabonds

Ah, the life of a vagabond—
We choose to be the mad ones,
don't you think?
Must keep choosing it,
lest the madness
Slip
through our twirling hands
and leave us with
Mundanity.

———

What do pirates and vagabonds have in common? A lot. Neither have a fixed abode. Neither like to follow the rules. Neither live conventional lifestyles in which nice, neat love stories fit nicely and neatly. They are also rebels, fiercely independent, and perhaps individualistic to a fault. Madness—the good kind that makes for visionaries and artists and agents of change—runs through their veins. And they have made an intentional choice to live outside the narrow confines of proper society; they will not relinquish this choice without drawing blood. When they fall in love, it may: 1. End in disaster, 2. Develop into a cinema-worthy romance, or 3. Become a long, drawn-out drama appropriate for an unsuccessful novel.

Let's begin with the worst-case scenario. Heed these signs, dear vagabondess, because they will save you much heartache and suffering: They want you to change your lifestyle for them. They want to join your path before you are ready. They are intimidated by your freedom. They don't like to travel. They are bigoted or judgmental about foreign cultures or people. They insist that real love requires sacrifice. When a vagabondess falls for this kind of person, she is in for a difficult ride.

Best-case scenario? They share your values, your passion for travel and learning, your spirit of independence, and your love of life. They, too, have let their inner vagabond(ess) out to play. Things flow at a pace that feels comfortable for you (there is no right answer as to what that pace may be). You like the version of yourself that shines brightly in this relationship. You make each other better, more open, more adventurous. You grow along the same path, for a time. They make a movie about your brilliant journey of love and vagabonding, a la *Pirates of the Caribbean*, but with less rum and more philosophy. This love story may take your breath away, but every movie has to end.

And the third possibility falls somewhere along the middle. It isn't earth-shattering, in a good or bad way. There is respect and humor along with obstacles and misunderstandings. It is like any relationship, anywhere, between any two human beings: messy, challenging, and ultimately filled with lessons that leave you better, wiser, stronger, or softer than you were before. This is the kind of connection that may last a long time. One with "space in your togetherness." It's not perfect, but nothing real ever is.

What kind of love story do you want to live? All three scenarios will teach you valuable lessons and enrich your journey; there is no wrong choice here. When they tell the story of your life as a vagabondess, who will fill the pages? Will they be a paragraph, a chapter, or part of the whole book? Will you be part of theirs? It's up to you.

⁓

"Let there be spaces in your togetherness, And let the winds of the heavens dance between you. Love one another but make not a bond of love: Let it rather be a moving sea between the shores of your souls. Fill each other's cup but drink not from one cup. Give one another of your bread but eat not from the same loaf. Sing and dance together and be joyous, but let each one of you be alone, Even as the strings of a lute are alone though they quiver with the same music. Give your hearts, but not into each other's keeping. For only the hand of Life can contain your hearts. And stand together, yet not too near together: For the pillars of the temple stand apart, And the oak tree and the cypress grow not in each other's shadow."—Kahlil Gibran

Lessons on Holding Lightly

May 2017, Portugal

I want to write about this thing I see in the traveling community—well, maybe it's my whole generation. It is a feeling more than a thing. I felt it cascading from the young hotel owner in Morocco who claimed to have slept with over 500 women. It permeated the hostel bar in Porto where I overheard a man speak with icy detachment of his ex-wife. These men, and women too, who appear to simultaneously seek and denounce meaning, especially in intimate relationships.

If I had to give this feeling a color, it would be a sepia brown. A note? E-minor. A smell… empty wine glasses, recently used and not yet clean. It lodges itself in sidelong glances. It gnaws at the gut as fingers twine guilelessly. It makes itself known in a kiss that says more than just "I want you," yet no one looks it in the face.

This nagging feeling whispers a truth we do not wish to hear: It is not enough, freedom. It is not enough, "free love." It is not enough, this pretending not to need. We yearn. A humming in E-minor chants, "more, more." The hope, barely masked: that there might be color. That this time, this time it might mean something.

＊

Love, when you are a vagabondess, comes and goes. Or, even if love stays, you come and go. I have never met a better teacher in detachment than the road of solo travel. "Let it go" has become a trite, near-meaningless catch-all for modern hippies, soccer moms, and millennials alike. Well before that song from *Frozen* came out, false Dalai Lama and Buddha quotes ran rampant through social media, and philosophy-lite truisms abounded in popular culture. All of it was telling us that to be happy, we just had to let go. Unfortunately, none of these Hallmark-style memes or celebrity sound bites did much to actually teach us how to do that. Rather, I would argue that they fueled the sepia-toned, melancholic search for meaning I started to observe in my fellow travelers a few years ago.

Here is a crash course in the Buddhist philosophy,

which, as far as I can tell, underpins our current cultural obsession with letting go. It begins with the Four Noble Truths: 1. Life involves suffering. 2. The cause of suffering is desire, or wanting things like pleasure or material goods. 3. To stop suffering, we must stop wanting those things. 4. In order to stop wanting and thus stop suffering, we must follow the Noble Eightfold Path. The eight elements of this path are Right Understanding, Right Thought, Right Speech, Right Action, Right Livelihood, Right Effort, Right Mindfulness, and Right Concentration. Now, if you really want to follow that path in the Buddhist way, welcome to the rest of your life. This is not the book for you. I'll just be touching on Truth number three and four.

There is a deceptive simplicity to the four truths outlined above. We suffer because we want things. In the context of love, we suffer because we are *attached* to our relationships working out in specific ways. That first date is going to be the story we tell our grandchildren about how we met. That gorgeous man sitting next to us at the bar is definitely going to ask us out. That person is going to be *our* person forever… and ever. When, inevitably, life happens and things work out differently, we suffer—in part because it sucks to not get what we want, sure, but mostly because we are attached to getting what we want, how we want it, when we want it. *Letting go,* then, is about softening our grip on those attachments and desires, so that when life inevitably happens and people exit our lives or relationships shift, it doesn't feel quite as catastrophic. (Trust me, I speak from a lifetime of experience wanting things to go *my* way. I have learned, am still learning, to soften my grip muscle by painful muscle.)

Saying the words doesn't make it so, however. The reason those Instagram memes and celebrity sound bites irk me so much is that they don't teach us anything about the *how*. How do we actually hold the things we love lightly? How do we get perspective on our desires, peeling back our fingers, one by one, and allowing the things we want to rest in our palm, rather than grasping them in our fist?

I'm not a Buddhist, and I'm by no means an expert on spiritual enlightenment. I'm just a vagabondess who has learned a tiny bit about attachment and suffering by experimenting with her own heart. I find it instructive to consider the philosophical foundations of this whole non-attachment thing, but it is in practice—trial and error—that I have tasted what it might be like to truly embody these principles.

When a vagabondess falls in love, she holds nothing back. So at home in solitude, she does not fear the possibility of "ending up alone." Perhaps it is because of this that she doesn't worry so much about whether or not a new relationship will work out, if they are "the one," or "where things are going." She has a lot of practice living in the present moment, allowing the future to unfold as it wishes. A vagabondess knows that, as the old adage goes, "If you want to make God laugh, tell him your plans." So she is content to plan little and enjoy her path as it unfolds. When love appears on that path, she tries to enjoy it too, without falling into the trap of clinging to a particular vision for the future. It's rarely as easy as it sounds, and she suffers anyway. But she learns and softens a little bit more through each cycle of holding and letting go.

Solo travel teaches us a lot about holding lightly, if we pay attention. It teaches us to be flexible about our plans, surrendering to unforeseen and unforeseeable obstacles like road closures, stomach bugs, and missed connections. It shows us, rather than telling us, that when we become attached to our plans, we are destined for disappointment and frustration. And finally, it immerses us into a present moment experience so rich and vivid, we do not want to dwell on half-formed things like "past" and "future." With time, a vagabondess may begin to integrate these lessons, soften her grip, and surrender to what is without clinging to what-may-come.

> "The only thing that is ultimately real about your journey is the step that you are taking at this moment. That's all there ever is."—Alan Watts

That said, a vagabondess is as human as anyone else. She grapples with doubt, fear, indecisiveness, expectation, disappointment, and insecurity. Taking your life on the road will not make any of these human attributes disappear. It will only give you a few new tools for managing or transforming them.

Through the Fear

> "Fear keeps us focused on the past or worried about the future. If we can acknowledge our fear, we can realize that right now we are okay. Right now, today, we are still alive…"
> —Thich Nhat Hanh

I remember my first serious heartbreak. I remember exactly what the carpet felt like beneath my open palm. I remember the floral pattern of the futon against the wall in front of me and the heat of the summer sun pouring through the window. I remember the baffling feeling of numbness that trailed me for days, maybe weeks.

I think the earth shattered a little bit that day for me. The details hardly matter; many years have passed in the interim, so you can fill in the gaps with your earth-shattering experience of choice.

That day, everything changed. My plans to head back to East Africa. My plans to move to Europe, or back to the U.S.—or anywhere. My entire conception of my future life. The shape of my heart. The certainty of the ground beneath me. Everything.

I hopped off my return flight in Amsterdam and flew to Italy instead. Don't get too excited, there was nothing *Eat. Pray. Love.* about it. I made my way to a small Sicilian town, and then another, and over the weeks that followed, I started to write. Words flowed like tears, like blood; through them, I came to understand my pain, my anger, and my grief. And slowly—very slowly—I began to shift.

The sky opened. For the first time, I understood the power of a broken heart. Carting my backpack (my life) and my laptop (my work), I wandered through eight countries—Italy, England, Sweden, Finland, Holland, South Africa, Uganda, Israel—getting back in touch with my nomadic soul. Beginning in those anonymous Sicilian streets, I became brave in my vulnerability, giving my story away freely. I didn't hide my heartbreak or bafflement; I harnessed it… or tried to.

"Vulnerability is not weakness. I define vulnerability as emotional risk, exposure, uncertainty. It fuels our daily lives."—Brene Brown

The volume, the intensity of the connections that came of this practice left me reeling: My friend's neighbor who looked me in the eyes and saw my truth written across them, and showed me his. The stranger in the airport who offered his story when I offered mine. The myriad humans who emerged from the woodwork to hold me, bolster me, and encourage my budding pair of fresh wings.

I embraced transparency, grace, fearlessness, and joy as the underpinnings of my journey moving forward. I continue to dedicate my life to those themes. Since then, I have felt my strength differently. I know just how uncertain my certainties are. I know how woefully unprotected my heart is. And yet, I welcome risk. I jump, knowing that the ground may or not be there when I land. I don't shy away from fear, anger, or the potential for disappointment.

I try to open myself to everything—love, heartbreak, pain, pleasure, fear, flight—and most of the time, everything opens right back.

I could tell you so many things that you have heard before. About how endings are really beginnings. About how light sneaks in through the cracks, and how scars are beautiful. That is all gloriously true.

But more than that, I want you to know, dear vagabondess, that pain is a tool, and it is a powerful one. When our hearts break, we can close them back together and seal them with cement—or we can leave them open.

There are seeds of joy in everything. When the earth shatters—a little bit—those seeds can find soil in which to grow. All we have to do is water them. I found my water; I don't know what yours is, but I know, absolutely, that it exists. There is a reason the symbol of the phoenix captivates us still. There is a reason we love the lotus. We, too, have wings that open when we least expect it. We, too, grow out of—in spite of, because of—thick, muddy challenges.

The Greatest Risk of All

As discussed in Chapter 1, we are all choosing our risks, all the time. What we eat, how we care for our bodies, where we live, and what we do—all of it comes with unique challenges and rewards. If you choose the path of a vagabondess, you choose the risks inherent in solo travel. But perhaps the greatest risk of all has nothing to do with motorcycle accidents, parasites, or assault.

The greatest risk of all touches the heart. Simply put, falling in love is scary. Trusting someone to carry our heart is terrifying. Opening up, getting vulnerable, and dropping our masks in an intimate relationship? Almost paralyzing! It's okay. As a vagabondess, you are choosing a practice of looking your fears in the face, acknowledging their presence, and moving through them in spite of it all. Fear and pain can paralyze us, or it can galvanize us into living a more courageous life.

Courage is not fearlessness. Courage describes a heart-centered path of action in the face of fear. Love is scary, and that's okay. The possibility of heartbreak is scary, and that's okay. We have two options in the face of fear: Turn back, or move forward. A vagabondess feels her fear, and she falls anyway. You, too, can harness the power of your deepest fears and embrace the loves that touch your path.

"Life is either a daring adventure or nothing."
—Helen Keller

It is August of 2018, and I have traveled to rural New York to train with twenty-eight women to become an Empowerment Self-Defense (ESD) instructor. We cover the map for every demographic: ages nineteen to seventy-five, thirteen countries, a dozen states, and people with zero martial arts training sitting beside Olympic athletes. Our passion for making the world safer—for women, for children, for everyone—has brought us together in an intense week of learning, training, and growing.

The second-to-last night of the ESD Global Self-Defense training, we have a board-breaking ceremony.

I never thought I would break a board. To be honest, it was so far outside the realm of possibility that before this night I never even considered whether or not I could.

I can, and I do. It feels powerful, raw, necessary… and inevitable.

The board is really just a symbol of the many problems we are breaking down through this work in empowerment self-defense: violence, oppression, injustice, control, fear. It's that last one that really gets me worked up. Violence causes incalculable harm, but fear erases entire worlds of possibility. When a woman is assaulted, what enrages me most are the comments blaming her: "She had no business traveling alone." "She shouldn't have been on the beach at night." Bullshit.

Traveling sisters and vagabondesses the world over, don't let these words in. Don't let doubt in. Don't let fear in. We have every right to travel alone. We have every right to inhabit public spaces at any time of day or night. We have every right to total, uncompromised safety.

Even if you are drunk, an assault is not your fault. Even if you are naked, an assault is not your fault.

Your decision to experience the world as a young, old, or somewhere-in-the-middle person full of life and curiosity should and does not mean you are to blame for anyone who might wish to do you harm because of it.

Traveling solo, I refuse to erase even a single possibility from my world. Dear vagabondess, I hope you may do the same.

They try to break us, but they forget how strong the earth is. How goddamn strong the sea is. How fucking indestructible the moon and her daughters are.

One day, we will live in a world where no one wishes to cause us harm for our gender, race, religion, ethnicity, or sexuality. I believe in that future, but I do not believe it is imminent. In the meantime, I break this board for my travel sisters, who have every right to move through this world without fear.

I teach ESD because waiting for change is too dangerous.

I do this work for you, sisters.

And I am doing this work for myself. Because to do nothing is to be complicit in my own disempowerment as a traveler, a woman, and a human being.

VIII. Staying Safe

Boundaries, Self-Defense, & The Dark Goddess

THIS CHAPTER COULD GO a lot of different ways. Conventional wisdom tells you not to wear revealing clothing, to watch your drinks, and to never, ever go into a stranger's home. Conventional wisdom also tells you to simply not travel alone while ignoring the fact that women are at greater risk at home than anywhere else (see Chapter 1), so let's just leave that all to the side and take this in another direction. (Of course, it is a good idea to watch your drinks, and I generally am in favor of dressing appropriately according to the values of your host culture.)

If you want someone to tell you that traveling solo is too dangerous, you have your mom, partner, or best friend. I would rather discuss practical tools for staying safe anywhere, for those of you who have already decided not to listen and to go and see. Keep in mind that I write this now as a trained empowerment self-defense instructor; however, I traveled solo for many, many years without any self-defense training at all. A self-defense course is an excellent option if you want to gain more confidence—and shed fear—before hitting the road. Still, given my own history, I don't feel that I can justifiably insist on it.

The following pages contain a summary of what I consider to be some of the simplest, most effective techniques to stay safe as a solo female traveler. Remember: A vagabondess does not need any fancy apps or gadgets. She carries all of her tools with her already: her voice, her body, her brain, her intuition, and her heart.

Intuition

We have already explored intuition in some depth in Chapter 3, so I don't want to dwell too long on it here. In summary: Trust your gut. If something feels wrong, it probably is. Trust your heart. If you feel like you can trust someone, you probably can. Trust your body. Feelings of tension or adrenaline signal danger. Feelings of relaxation or calm signal safety. You know more than you know. In many ways, solo travel demands radical self-reliance on your own knowing, so get in the habit of listening to and trusting it.

Boundaries (Find Your NO; Live Your YES)

Considering possible anecdotes to share in this section, I came to a sad realization: There are simply too many to choose. You want a story about being followed in a strange city? I have a dozen. You want a story about a stranger at a bar never get-

ting the message that I'm not interested? I have hundreds. You want to hear about all the ways a woman's body, space, and boundaries are disrespected on a sometimes daily basis? Just ask a woman close to you, or step outside and pay attention.

Dear vagabondess, you probably know only too well that harassment is an unforgivably common part of the female experience. In their frequency, these stories have become unremarkable. Not even one stands out to me and asks to be shared. However, just because we have normalized this behavior, that does not mean it is in any way acceptable. We have the opportunity to practice setting and standing up for our boundaries in small ways every single day. I believe we must do so, or risk complacency in our own oppression.

A vagabondess should quickly get comfortable with saying no: "No, I don't need a taxi." "No, I don't want a guide." "No, thank you, that's beautiful, but I don't want to buy it." It can be a "no" with a smile, or a "no, but thank you so much." However, if the message isn't getting across with gentle, polite communication, sometimes you have to be more assertive: "I said no," on repeat, with an even, low tone of voice and strong posture, usually gets results.

Unfortunately, just about anywhere you go in the world, a woman's "no" doesn't receive the same immediate respect as a man's. Nevertheless, "no" is a complete sentence, requiring neither apology nor explanation. Do not fall into the trap of negotiating over your no, or you will end up spending time, money, and energy on conversations, things, and people you don't actually want.

Of course you *can* apologize or explain *if you want to.* The point, as I am constantly reminding students in my self-defense classes, is that it's a choice, not an obligation.

When dealing with harassment—unwanted touch, flirtation, or other behavior—a similar technique works well. Choose one line (e.g. "I don't want to talk right now." "Do not touch me." "Leave me alone.") and stick with it. There is no need to shout or get defensive unless the harasser becomes more threatening. Again, a low, even tone, confident body language, and a refusal to enter into any negotiations (but why? Come on... I'm just being nice, etc.) can put a stop to a lot of unwanted behaviors.

An alternative involves "naming" the behavior we want to change or stop. This is one of my favorite ESD (Empowerment Self-Defense) techniques.

1. We first **name the behavior** (e.g. "Your hand is on my leg." "You're staring at me." "You're following me.") without questions or qualifications. Questions invite response, denial, or negotiation. In a dangerous or uncomfortable situation, we don't want to start a conversation or argue over the facts; we just want to make the necessary changes to feel safe.
2. After naming the behavior, we **state the change** we wish to see (e.g. "Stop touching me." "Leave me alone.") without feeling obliged to ask nicely or say please. If once is not enough, we can return to repetition until the message lands.

I love this technique for several reasons. First, it leaves no room for doubt; we both know what's going on here, and we're not going to argue over that. Second, it alerts any bystanders to the situation. We'll come back to that in the following section on seeking help. Finally, it clearly states a boundary: "You're doing this. I don't want you to. Stop." If the behavior persists, we then know a person does not respect our boundaries or care about our needs.

As a vagabondess, you must be prepared to speak up when someone crosses a line. This can become more complex with cultural relativism. If everyone in your destination greets with a kiss on both cheeks, but you hate physical contact with strangers, what do you do? While it is good to push beyond your comfort zone and engage with an unfamiliar culture as much as possible, a hard no is still a hard no. Keep in mind, if simply being in a culture violates your boundaries, it is up to you to choose another destination, adjust your plans, or otherwise take into account your responsibility in the matter. For instance, if you need a lot of personal space, you should not take public transport in India, East Africa, or most of the world for that matter. If you do then choose to take public transport, you are consenting to be in a very crowded space, squished in with a lot of other bodies belonging to people you have never met. (You are not, by any means, consenting to harassment or assault.)

Particularly for women traveling alone, harassment can be a serious issue. It is entirely possible—and necessary!—to communicate and enforce boundaries with respect and grounded assertiveness. It may feel uncomfortable at first. That's okay. It gets easier. You'll probably even start to enjoy your newfound no-nonsense communication style after a while. Again, *of course* there are other, more conventional ways to avoid harassment, such as never going anywhere alone. But, dear vagabondess, is that how you want to spend your life? You have a right to move through the world without the socially mandated protection of a travel companion or partner. You have a right to define and defend your boundaries, regardless of who is walking beside you—if anyone.

If the situation calls for it, you may also want to turn up the volume. Yelling has been shown to prevent as many as 50% of assaults against women. The voice is a powerful self-defense tool. To yell effectively, be sure to use your belly—singers, actors, and public speakers will already know how to do that—to protect your vocal chords and bring more power and resonance to your voice. I highly encourage you to try this at home! Tell your neighbors you're taking an acting class (this explains everything), grab a few friends, blast some music, and practice shouting "NO!" as loud as you can. Remember to yell from your center; it can be helpful to keep your hands on your belly as a tactile reminder when practicing.

People who attack, assault, or harass other people are not superhumans. They are vulnerable to someone shouting in their face, the shame of being called out publicly, or (to bring us to our next section), the pain of a palm heel strike to the nose. While it should never, ever be anyone's responsibility to avoid assault or harassment—and a victim is never, ever to blame for their assault—this is the world we live in. Whether close to home or abroad, a vagabondess should be prepared to take her safety into her own hands. This, too, is part of the creed of self-reliance.

Physical Self-Defense

"Being able to defend myself is not violence. It is a human right! It's MY right."
—Yehudit Zicklin-Sidikman, Founder & President, ESD Global

A book is not the place for physical self-defense training. If you feel called to learn how to connect with your physical power, I recommend seeking out Empowerment Self-Defense or IMPACT self-defense courses in your area. Martial arts such as jiu jitsu, krav maga, judo, and muay thai also provide good training for self-defense purposes.

For now, suffice it to say that you have the strength you need to keep yourself safe, regardless of your size, age, or fitness level. Think about the hard, protected parts of your body as weapons: heel of the hand, elbow, knee, hips, feet, voice. Think about the soft, vulnerable parts of an attacker's body as targets: face, nose, gut, genitals, tops of the feet, knees, shins, eyes. If it is not possible to avoid a physical altercation (i.e. communicating strong boundaries and/or shouting does not put an end to the threat; it is not possible to leave the situation and get to safety; your best option is to stay and fight), then bring all of your power to those weapons that you carry in your body. Your basic survival instincts will take you far; of course, additional training in martial arts techniques doesn't hurt, either!

Body Language

I am an expert at looking like I know exactly where I am going, even when I am hopelessly lost. Friends who have traveled with me can confirm that. However, when it comes to staying safe as a solo traveler, I actually think this is an excellent skill to cultivate. Confident body language—shoulders back, head up, relaxed pace, alert gaze—signals to anyone around us that we are aware of our surroundings, at ease, and confident in our power. In a dangerous situation, we can bring our hands up, fingers wide, in a gesture of "stop/back off" to signal to a would-be attacker that this is our space and we are prepared to defend it.

Any potential danger aside, I recommend cultivating posture and body language that communicates ease and confidence. If the world expects a woman traveling alone to be scared and small, be fearless and big. If threatening people on the street expect you to be meek and quiet, be bold and loud. In any situation, taking up space is a simple and effective way to declare that we will hold our ground and that we are not afraid to be here.

Additional ways to move like a vagabondess: Keep your phone in your bag or pocket when walking around. Nothing says, "I'm not paying attention," like walking with your nose to your screen. Observe your surroundings, keeping your eyes open and taking in as much information as you can. (Incidentally, this is also a great technique for travel writers or photographers!) Avoid listening to music or otherwise creating a barrier between you and your surroundings; stay aware and alert. Relax! You're here to enjoy and connect. It's only necessary to enter into a defensive mode if you feel threatened. Your resting state can be free of tension—relaxed alertness only.

We work with boundaries and self-defense so that we *can* relax and open to the world, not to shut ourselves up in high, impenetrable towers. But in order to truly say "yes" to the connections, conversations, and experiences you *do* want, you must be able to say "no," confidently, to the things you don't want. Knowing that you can and will defend your boundaries, you can really, wholeheartedly enjoy your journey without nagging fears lingering in the back of your mind.

Asking for Help

If you feel unsafe, seek support. One of my favorite methods for dealing with harassment in public spaces involves seeking help from a specific individual. When many people are present, crowd psychology can often take over if you solicit help from the collective: "Oh, someone else will help her." "There are so many people here, why should it be me?" Instead, if you feel threatened by somebody's behavior, try choosing one person who seems like they may be willing to help you, look them in the eyes, and say, "I need help," or, "I need support."

Alternatives: "This person is bothering me, can you switch seats with me?" "This person is touching me, can you please help?" "This person is following me, could you walk with me back to my hotel?" "I feel unsafe. I need support."

If the first person you go to is unwilling or unable to provide the support you need, go to someone else. Generally speaking, however, it is much more difficult to ignore someone's request for help when it is directed specifically at you. Remember: Most people are good, kind, and caring. If you feel you are in danger and there are people around, appeal to that basic goodness.

Asking for help is one of the simplest ways to stay safe when traveling solo. Want to avoid getting lost in a new city at night? Ask directions from the nice lady sitting next to you on the train. She may even offer to drop you off. Don't feel comfortable with your hostel roommates? Seek support from the woman at reception and see if you can change rooms. Think someone is following you? Go into the nearest cafe and ask if you can sit for a while until they leave or if someone can walk with you. Or go up to the next person you pass on the street and explain what's happening.

Most people are good, kind, and caring. To be a vagabondess requires a certain degree of optimism and faith in that statement. While the risks of solo travel are real, they are not the whole picture. They are not even a tiny corner of the picture. The picture is beautiful, with a few sketchy edges. Self-defense is about being prepared for those moments of ugliness, rare though they may be.

The Darker Archetypes

Finally, I believe there is an element of unlearning conditioned behaviors behind this work in self-defense and solo travel. *Girls should always be polite. Girls shouldn't yell, or fight, or show aggression. Girls should defer to the desires of men. Girls shouldn't get angry.* The foundational pillars of the patriarchy, in short.

There is a place for politeness, kindness, softness, and gentleness. When I feel safe and at ease, I prefer to live and relate with an open heart and a big smile. However, when we teach girls to never fight, never get angry, never say no, never be wild, we raise a generation of women who struggle to defend themselves—women who *cannot* yell, fight, and raise hell when their survival depends on it.

Self-defense and solo travel both teach us to unlearn some of the "truths" society instills in us from a young age. We unlearn the trope of "it's too dangerous," and learn that we can, in fact, do it alone. We unlearn our fear of the world and learn to trust—our own intuition, and the basic goodness of others. We unlearn the age-old stereotype that a woman's place is at home, and we learn to claim our space in the big, wide world "out there."

And last but not least, we unlearn the giant lie that the only way to be feminine is to be soft, deferential, and accommodating. If the default archetype for many women today is the girlish maiden or the nurturing mother, then in self-defense work, we learn to reclaim the darker feminine archetypes: the witch, the destructive goddess, the wild woman, the warrior. In channeling our natural aggression—our inner warrior woman—toward healing and growth, we become more integrated.

In embracing this lifestyle of self-reliance, we celebrate our agency, for the vagabondess is sovereign unto herself. In adopting a spirit of incorrigible optimism, we connect with the open heart of the child—ready to love and embrace the world for all its contradictions.

When we embrace both the warrior and the vaga-bondess—aggression and open-heartedness—we unite two aspects of our own psyche that have too often been twisted, broken down, or hidden away deep in the recess-es of our subconscious along with all the other beautiful things we demonize. When we give space to these two women, we step into profound integration. We heal. And when one of us heals, we all heal.

This is what I believe this lifestyle is all about.

- 2016 -

What are you searching for?

I see the questions in your smile, and I am curious. Tender.

Tell me your sadness, for whose sake you wander while yearning for home. Tell me your emptiness, which you have tried to fill 500 times.

It is written on your face, but I don't want to read your story—I want to listen to it.

Take your time; we're in no rush.

Close your eyes and rest your head on my shoulder, there, and tell me your longing. (I won't answer it—not me—but I can be your witness.)

Roll slowly along the heartbreaks and weave through the disappointments; trace your words across the echoes, the hollows, the hopes. Step sweetly into your history, and let me follow, please.

You are looking at my joy as if it were a destination, but I have painted my soul with its unique palette, and you must choose your own colors.

I see you hovering on the wanting, but you don't ask; I watch you balancing against the seeking, but you don't reach; I hear you edging closer to the yearning, but you gild it in false fulfillment and do not touch its source.

Ask—ask the questions flickering at the corners of your eyes. Ask me about joy.

I will take your hand, and I will lead you back—past the heartbreaks and the disappointments, beyond the echoes, the hollows, the hopes—back to your beginning, which you long to reach but don't know how.

And this time, you will not linger at the threshold. This time, you will step inside.

And I will leave you there, alone to paint your joy with the colors only your soul can know. Choose well.

IX. The Inner Journey

I Die, Therefore I Live

September, 2014. Southern Vermont, U.S.A.

It can't be nine o'clock when my fire goes out. It was a sad excuse for a bonfire anyway. Night quickly crowds in. Icy beads of dew form upon the rocks. The stars rise. I unroll my emergency blanket and lie down by the embers, but it is useless. The cold from the earth seeps through to my bones. I have left my sleeping bag and other gear snug under a tarp at my base camp, unreachable in the dark. I march in circles— endless circles—to keep warm. I stop when I can and huddle beneath my blanket, but the moment my eyes close the cold wakes me back up, and I start marching again.

I am not lost in the woods, nor am I suffering through survival training. No, no. This is the last night of my vision quest, a voluntary four-day, four-night solo fast.

―――

IN NEARLY EVERY SPIRITUAL TRADITION, we can find evidence of prophets, hermits, and regular curious people going alone into nature—without sustenance—to seek spirit, or something like it. Jesus and Siddhartha are only the most famous examples. Anthropologists coined the term "vision quest" to describe the Native American rite of passage; however, the broader practice has roots in many, many cultures and belongs to none. I could not have comfortably participated, twice, had this not been the case.

Traditionally, on the fourth night of a vision quest, one might hope, beg or cry for a vision. In my first quest, however, I am merely hoping not to freeze. After four days without food, I do not enjoy an elevated state of consciousness as I had expected. I only feel weak and cold. The stars swim before my eyes, forming briefly, I am certain, the shape of a dragonfly. Every few laps of my self-made enclosure, I stop to gaze across the lake, toward the east where the sun will surely rise soon. It can't be midnight when I start to imagine soft rays of light above the mountains, eager heralds of dawn.

I think it was reading Murakami's *Kafka on the Shore* that did it. As Kafka entered the forest and met himself in nature, my imagination followed, and my body yearned to do the same. I wouldn't say Murakami's words planted the seed, which was planted long before, but they undoubtedly watered it. Suddenly, I found myself Googling "vision quest Vermont" and scrolling through the search results, pining after... what? A vacation? I was certainly tired of work. A vision? Nothing so lofty. Relaxation? Definitely not. I could think of nothing more challenging than spending four days and nights without food. Insight? Clarity? Purpose? Something like that.

I found the idea of meeting myself in nature—the philosophical underpinnings of the modern-day vision fast—deeply compelling. I sought that which demanded solitude, surrender, and tenacity. What that was, I wasn't quite sure. Even now I'm not sure I could provide much more insight, though I have spent much time in the intervening years seeking that something.

And so at dawn on September 18, 2014, I rose from a night of wide-eyed restlessness and set out for Putney, Vermont, a two-hour drive south. I listened to pop music and VPR on rotation to drown out my mind's chattering. Predictions on the Scottish election accompanied me out of my daily life and into the liminal space of my ten-day program.

My idyllic expectations (vague though they were) of my solo time quickly collided with reality. I did not frolic in the lake, but dashed in and out instead, shivering beneath the weak September sun for an hour afterwards. Wholly unglamorous sightings of ducks and dragonflies supplanted my dreams of close encounters with deer and wolves. Days, I discovered, are unbelievably long when there is nothing to do. I went to bed before the sun, exhausted by the nothingness and ready to move on to the next day. I was hungry. Always.

In the dark, dry leaves falling to the ground sounded like the scampering of a hundred tiny feet. Sightless and marooned in my sleeping bag, I fancied all the creatures of the forest sidling closer to spy on me in my sleep. I was not scared, but neither was I free and resplendent in my solitude. Weary and alone, I learned to talk to trees to pass the time.

At last, the darkness lifts from the ordeal of my final night, and I return to my gear and walk away laboriously, stopping often to catch my breath. I carry a walking stick that I have, in my ample free time, decorated with stones and colored yarn symbolic of particular experiences. Rocks.

Metaphorically speaking, however, my hands are empty. I feel like I have somehow failed. So much time, so much effort to come so far, and for what? I don't know what I have learned. They say a vision quest lasts a year. In the months that follow, I will turn those perplexing days over and over in my mind, trying to answer that question: How do we return when we have nothing to show for our journey?

I brought back nothing. And maybe that was the point.

I completed my first vision fast in 2014, at the age of twenty-two. Four days and four nights alone in the forests of Vermont—and very hungry. I completed my second vision fast recently, in January of 2019. Three days and three nights alone in the jungles of Costa Rica—and not so hungry. I still find the idea of meeting myself in nature, stripped of every routine and comfort of daily life, extremely compelling.

What could drive someone to set out into the wilderness for four days with no food or shelter? Why would anyone drink a sticky brew of jungle vines that induces extreme purging and sometimes hallucinations? What drives human beings to forsake society and ignore every instinct of survival, procreation, or pleasure in favor of a life of extreme scarcity in a remote mountain cave? What grand prize could be waiting on the other side that we are so willing to walk through fire, scale mountains, battle monsters, and confront dark nights of the soul to get there?

We humans are, by nature, relentless seekers. We crave truth. We yearn for magic. We pine after knowing. We seek that elusive "something" out there, even though we know that the truth and magic and knowledge we truly desire reside within. We walk for hundreds of miles, fast for days, cross oceans and deserts, and spend years in the searching. We are seeking adventure, connection, and novelty, certainly. But more than anything, all that time, I believe we are seeking ourselves.

And yet, the outer journey is not in vain, for it leads us to our path of inner discovery. Just as we leave footprints in the earth behind us, the earth marks us in return with faint but unmistakable trails, mapping the route we must follow inward. Each place we visit offers another clue: Here, you learned how to mark time counting your breaths, for there was nothing else. Here, you learned the language of trees. Here, you learned what your laugh sounds like when no one is listening. Keep going; you're on the right path.

Maybe you wouldn't use the words I do, but I suspect that if the path of the vagabondess calls to you, then you, too, are curious about going "out there" to meet yourself. Excellent. Now that we've addressed many of the practical questions, fears, and doubts common to those starting out on this path, maybe you have a bit more mental space to consider the layer beneath: the inner journey.

I can't tell you how your inner journey should unfold, or where it might lead you. Let me make this clear: I have no idea where you have been or where you are going. I just have a few ideas (I think they're pretty good ones) about how to connect with that process. It's easy to coast along the surface level of our experience, but I challenge you to dive deep.

It may be more pleasant to ignore the reality of the world—this includes death, illness, inequity, and all variety of darkness—but I encourage you to examine the full spectrum of experience present in this existence. It is certainly less complicated to keep our attention focused outward, never examining the messy, chaotic, beautiful collection of emotions, desires, fears, and patterns we carry within, but I dare you to choose the more difficult route and journey within, even as you venture without.

> "Whatever I have learned about the nature of the self […] has been by going inward and down into the fruitful darkness […] The most important secrets seem always to hide in the shadows. "The secret of life," say the Utes, "is in the shadows and not in the open sun; to see anything at all, you must look deeply into the shadow of a living thing." "—Joan Halifax

Get Deeper

You will not find a tally of countries I've visited anywhere on my website or Instagram—or in this book, for that matter. I've debated changing my policy about this, as it seems to be *de rigueur* for writers and bloggers in my niche of adventure travel and digital nomadism. I am proud of the ground I've managed to cover in relatively few years. However, I'm much prouder of *how* I've covered it.

From the start, I have wanted to tell real stories about my years on the road, which numbers can never do justice. Numbers may tell you how many kilometers I walked, how many years I lived out of a backpack, or—yes—how many stamps I have in my passport. But numbers won't tell you what the Phnom Penh pavement felt like under my dirty feet, how my shoulders ached after carrying my life with me across Spain, or the many amusing (stressful) ways I crossed all those borders.

The number of countries I have visited is, like any other tally, just a number. It is not, in my opinion, very interesting information. (Incidentally, I feel the same about age, nationality, astrological signs, and many other pieces of information that supposedly reveal so much yet also reveal nothing.) What's more, it is already an exceptional privilege to travel as I have done, as discussed in the introduction. I am deeply grateful for my lifestyle and all the opportunities that brought me to it. It seems unnecessary to flaunt that privilege in such a one-dimensional way.

I also dislike the rhetoric, only too common in the travel blogosphere, that "more countries = more happy." There is no happiness equation. A fuller passport does not equate to a higher happiness index, though travel can certainly lead us down many paths to fulfillment. I am wary of contributing to this superficial conversation in any way. Yet, when I tell new friends about my vagabondish lifestyle, more often than not their first question is, "So, how many countries have you been to?" And so

I've come up with a lot of ways to avoid, or transform, that question. I offer you a few of my favorites:

1. "Let me tell you about my most recent trip to X." Stays on topic, but narrows the conversation down to a specific, less superficial angle that I actually want to explore.
2. "A lot... I've been living nomadically for quite a few years." Vague, but hopefully avoids anything that might come off as boasting.
3. "Honestly, I'd rather answer a different question." The most direct answer, and usually goes over well when delivered with a genuine smile.
4. "I actually don't think it's that interesting. Let me tell you a story instead." Also direct, and opens space for the exchange to move toward a subject of mutual interest.
5. Just tell them the number. Once in a while, it's easier to go with the flow and answer the damn question.

I like these answers because most of them are rather versatile. The same tactics can help us to gracefully evade personal questions we don't want to answer, small talk we don't want to engage in, and norms of conversation we don't want to support.

My challenge to you, then, dear vagabondess, is this: Go deeper. Go beyond numbers—age, birthday, salary, stamps in your passport. Dig beneath the small talk, so beloved of backpackers and cocktail party hostesses, and pull up the damp, fragrant earth underneath. Talk about your fears, your near-death experiences, your personal philosophy (even if it's still half-baked), and your gods. Talk about your dreams and heartbreaks and disappointments. Break the "politics, money, religion" rule, and talk about all the taboo things proper society hides. Or even if you don't talk about it, *think about it*.

I challenge you, vagabondess or vagabondess-to-be, to *go deeper*. You can plan your trip around numbered lists of must-dos and must-sees on travel forums, Buzz-Feed, or the *New York Times*—and that's perfectly fine. But why stop there? As you plan and dream and wander, consider your inner journey, too.

Will I grow? This is the critical question to ask. Personal growth is not a mathematical equation. X Countries + X Years of Travel does not equal Wisdom. Self-actualization is not a place on the map. The inner journey plods onward, no matter where we are. Our movement through physical space, at its purest and perhaps most exalted level, is a metaphor for our movement through the infinite cosmos contained within our own psyche. *What's in there? Don't you want to find out?*

The Archetypes Within

"People will do anything, no matter how absurd, in order to avoid facing their own souls. One does not become enlightened by imagining figures of light, but by making the darkness conscious."
—Carl Jung

What's scarier, a new country, or your own mind? Many people, faced with the choice to dig deep and confront their own monsters, or to evade that inner work and go traveling instead, will choose the latter. Unfortunately for you, that's a false choice. As we already discussed in Chapter 1, travel is not an escape from anything.

Travel is not an escape from the Self—not the kind of travel a vagabondess engages with anyway. Outward travel is just another path *inward*. Physical movement, adventure, wandering—these are all different roads to the same destination: you. Try as you might to avoid them, those dark inner caves, filled with personal myths and monsters, are waiting at the end of every trail, every transatlantic flight, and every soul-searching backpacking trip.

So, are you ready to meet yourself? I'm not a psychologist, but I have been a student of my own mind my entire life, and I've come to a few conclusions, which I think some psychologists share. I believe that we all contain a multitude of personalities, or archetypes, within us. While our "default mode" may tend toward certain traits, this does not mean we cannot consciously cultivate other facets of our Self that we deem valuable. For instance, as mentioned in Chapter 4, a classic "introvert" may choose to connect to qualities of extroversion as she travels solo, embracing elements of her personality that, although perhaps less natural, are nonetheless present and within reach.

Some of the archetypes I've personally cultivated include The Witch. The Child. The Vagabondess or Wanderer (of course). The Warrior. What does it mean to explore archetypal qualities as you travel? In brief, it means to play with your sense of self, giving space for different parts of your inner world to come out and express. It means being flexible with how you define yourself, understanding *you* as something fluid and constantly evolving, rather than cast from iron. It means observing how different selves come out in different contexts (e.g. Who are you when you're visiting your family? Who are you with your best friends? Who are you when you're alone in the woods?) and acknowledging that "you" are a shifting amalgamation of all of those selves. The result of this process of introspection can be profound, leading to a far more complex self-awareness and a practical adaptability that will serve you well in your travels.

Death & Surrender

"The fact of death is unsettling. Yet there is no other way to live."—Paul Kalanithi

August, 2016. Naples, Italy.

I will contemplate my death a hundred times today. Sharp turns and sudden stops. Engine hum in my bones and ocean wind in my hair. It is the last weekend of August, and my friend and his vintage motorcycle meet me at the Salerno train station a half-hour from Napoli. Along with crowds of Italian holiday-makers, we set off for the Amalfi Coast. Now, maybe hopping on a motorcycle sounds like a stupid risk to you; maybe you understand the allure. For me, every ride is a powerful metaphor for the precipice we all walk—every day of our lives.

The fresh wind in my face balances the hot sun as we follow hairpin turns opening onto one dazzling vista after another. The roar of the engine blends with the waves and the wind, and conversation is sparse. The sky turns to dusty rose, orange, teal, and we round past Amalfi and up the Sorrentino coast just in time for sunset.

An hour later, the headlights of oncoming traffic blur as we race down the centerline of the autostrada (highway) from Sorrento to Napoli. I settle into the peculiar flow of navigating traffic, weaving in and out.

Yellow lines, black sky, breathe in, breathe out.

Yellow lights, black tires, breathe in, breathe out.

Accelerate, brake. In. Out.

It is just me and my friend. Fear has hopped off this train.

I have contemplated my death a hundred times today. I usually do when I travel as a motorcycle passenger, and I don't think it's morbid. There's a zen quality to this process that renders it uniquely compelling for me. There's the "Oh shit, this is dangerous" moment, followed by the "There's nothing I can do to change my absolute vulnerability in this situation" realization, culminating in (temporary) total surrender to the inalterable fact of my own mortality.

Then a sudden acceleration and "oh shit," and we begin again. As the minutes or hours blur on, I slowly stop picturing the many gruesome ways in which things could end badly, my pulse slows, and my shoulders relax. Once that last ripple of fear smooths out, I enter a space of zen-ed out acceptance. It's pretty blissful there.

How often, in your day-to-day life, do you contemplate your own mortality? I'm guessing it's not all that often (and I will happily be wrong in my assumptions if you regularly meditate on the subject). Many modern cultures are deathly afraid of death, and the theme is considered unfit for polite conversation. It's not "healthy" to think about death, right? Wrong! It is unhealthy, in my opinion (and I think the Buddhists and the shamans and the psychologists will back me up on this), to suppress the other half of life. When we deny the fact of death, darkness, violence, aggression, pain, and all the other scary things we prefer not to look at, we stifle the complex reality of our existence.

We are all mortal. We are all helplessly vulnerable to myriad risks. We all walk a fine line between life and death all the time. We are all on a precipice. That yellow double line of a Napoletano highway, framed by black sky and black asphalt, is only a metaphor, no more and no less terrifying than the reality we all face. Every day. The magic of this "motorcycle zen" I so love is not the "added" risk. Rather, it forces me to reckon with the transience always enveloping me—always enveloping us—and to breathe in, breathe out, and enjoy the view.

Surrendering to the inherent danger of being alive, surrendering to the vulnerability of living in this fragile body and carrying this even more fragile heart, surrendering to the unavoidable truth that we won't be here forever—for me, this is the spiritual core of solo travel. It is in surrender that we release the choking fear, breathe deeply, and truly live. Until, of course, the fear strikes once more, and we get to do it all over again. A vagabondess lives this process countless times. I can't tell you that she grows wiser, or more enlightened, or even happier in the bargain, but one thing is certain: While she is alive, she is very much alive.

Contemplation

June, 2015. Northern Spain.

It's time. I close my laptop for a month. I put two pairs of pants, three shirts and a sleeping bag into my backpack, and I head to San Sebastian in the Northeast of Spain. I've been waiting for this day for a while now. I need a vacation. I need a total break from society. But if you haven't caught on yet, there are always layers to my reasoning. This is no exception.

I don't know why I want to walk the Camino de Santiago, an ancient pilgrimage trail leading across Spain to Santiago de Compostela. I just know that it calls to me; I know that this adventure is my way of seeking right now. I know that a search need not have an object. Sometimes, it is the act of searching that matters.

On the threshold of this journey, a memory floats up: As I prepared for my first vision quest, someone dear to me said, "I hope you find what you're looking for." I did not find it. I didn't know what I was looking for, and I still don't. I made the mistake then of thinking—hoping—I would discover in searching the reason for my search. In 2016, I have no such lofty aspirations.

There are the obvious motivations. Nature. Space to breathe. Air to think. A break—from work, from time, from everything. But that's all somewhat superficial. My true reasons run deeper, of this I am certain. I am as mystified by them as anyone, yet still I go.

To simply walk. To place one foot in front of the other. This is my task.

Dear vagabondess, I invite you to pursue your searches, your seeking, your quest without needing to know *why*. It doesn't matter where we go, for how long, or in search of what prize. What matters is that we walk. And that we look. This is as true for our inner path as it is for our outward wandering.

Just as we ask questions in the interest of taking a conscious approach to travel in the outer world (see Chapter 5), we can ask questions about our inner journey, to similar effect. The answer may end up being, "I don't care, I just want to enjoy the beach, dammit!" And that's okay. The answer may be a plaintive "I don't know!!!" That's also okay. The point is to ask. As an expert maker of lists, I feel inclined to divide up some of my key questions for introspection into the following categories:

1. Emotional body.
2. Intellectual stimulation.
3. Spiritual growth.

Here are my guiding questions for the inner journey of a vagabondess, which I hope may serve you, too:

How is my "emotional body?" What feelings are coming up for me in this situation? If I sit with those feelings, can I touch their source, and in so doing understand something more about myself? Why do I feel happy/sad/anxious/melancholic/ecstatic in this moment? Do I need to "do" something about my current emotional state, or can I simply allow it to be and then to pass? What do my emotions want to teach me? What lessons in impermanence, holding lightly, and releasing expectations are embedded in this emotional reaction? How can I take responsibility for my emotional body, despite the very human impulse to blame external factors?

At the level of intellect, what am I learning from this place, person, or experience? Can I soften my attachment to my worldview in order to try on this different perspective? If I release the need to be right in this disagreement, what can I learn from this vastly contrasting opinion, custom, or belief? Am I gathering new information here? How could I seek more information, better information, or deeper information about this place, person, or culture? Do I feel intellectually stimulated or challenged? If not, what actions could I take to ensure my continued learning and expansion?

At the level of spirit or soul, am I growing? What needs to shift so that I can continue to expand? Is it an inner shift, or something exterior? Is this place, person, or experience aligned with my intentions for spiritual growth? Why has this place, person, or experience crossed my path? How can this challenge, setback, or obstacle be an opportunity for growth or self-awareness? Do I feel open, alive, and receptive? How can I cultivate this state of being through my inner and outer environment? Do I feel closed, tired, or blocked? How can I move through that in order to expand even more?

Remember, the answers are secondary. I do not believe there is any intrinsic meaning in our experience that we will find if we seek long enough. I do believe that by asking questions—by seeking—we imbue our experience with meaning of our own making. The most important thing, then, is to ask.

> "I have been and still am a seeker, but I have ceased to question stars and books; I have begun to listen to the teaching my blood whispers to me."
> —Hermann Hesse

TALKING ABOUT GOD

I went to the ocean on a cloudy night, just to stare at
darkness.

I felt my heart beat faster as the waves rolled against the
beach,
and my body rolled, too, in sympathy.
This was solitude.
Utter blankness upon the canvas of my cornea.
This was emptiness.
Division between water and sky barely visible on the
horizon.

My voice, when I sang out to that ocean beat,
was unique in all the darkness,
for it was the only thing that told itself to itself.
The sea spoke to the moon,
the raindrops spoke to the trees,
the rocky beach spoke to the colonies of crickets—
and then, there was me.

I want so much to be a part of it.
To lose track of my voice in harmony with the waves.
To see my footprints disappear,
my skin melt into the everything
of that shifting, sucking darkness.

I love my life, my body, my breath.
Just, I want to be a part of it.
The whole.

You see, no one I know seems to be talking about god—
it's out of vogue to seek the divine,
the mysterious, the ethereal, and the invisible;
children learn to count money but hear nothing of
souls;
we don't care why we're here as long as there's football—

And no one I know seems to be talking about god;
we're all too educated for that,
leave it to the zealots and the black hats,
write your gratitude journal and bow down to the fat
cats—

No, no one I know seems to be talking about god,
but I want to find her,
so I go down to the water and look into my own heart,
because a wise teacher or two once said
I would find a spark—
there, where all the secret things we pretend not to believe in sing;
where the ancient longing we don't understand goes to
hide;
where the invisible and magical and wild abide.

I heard, once, that god was at the heart of everything,
including me.
I read, once, that gods played and ate and shifted faces
at the bottom of the sea.
I knew, once—
I knew, I knew, I knew, I knew, I knew—
about the mysteries dancing at the horizon,
where water meets sky,

about the spirits who live between worlds
and send stories with serpents and dolphins and
dragonflies,
about the beauty that gave birth to every single thing.

But I forgot,
we forgot,
and I want so much to remember:
I am part of it.

No one I know seems to be talking about god,
but, call me crazy,
I want to find her.
So every day, for a few minutes,
I try to stare at darkness.
I dive into that shifting, sucking water,
and I look into my own heart.

Conclusion

Go Out

IT IS THURSDAY, EARLY MORNING, late November in San Jose, Costa Rica. I have been writing every day for three weeks to arrive at this point. I sit at the kitchen counter in my studio apartment, looking out the window at the mountains to the south. Clear light filters through the curtains, which I own. My grandmother's scarf drapes haphazardly over the desk chair, which I own. I am alternately overwhelmed and humbled by the number of things that I own here. I glance at the exuberant plants tumbling over my desk, where I rarely sit, the bottles of kombucha fermenting in a shaded corner, the shelf of books I have collected in so little time, a small library. *So much accumulated,* I think. *I could never fit it all in one backpack.* Yet I hold it lightly. If there is one thing I have learned as a vagabondess, it is this.

There is no denying the beauty and allure of staying for a while. Friendships deepen into a different hue, one of constancy. Kitchen projects that require time and special ingredients can flourish. All those people who once opened their doors in welcome can now find sanctuary here, even if it means sleeping on the floor. All the energy I put into learning my way around a new place, meeting new people, getting acquainted with a new language and culture—right now I put it into building community, developing my brand, and driving forward creative projects like this book.

At the moment, I do not live "in community," although my network of friends and colleagues in this city is beautifully interwoven after two years of cultivating connections. My work consists of a dozen different projects at any given time, some the same digitally nomadic positions I've held for years, others retreats and workshops intimately rooted in this place. I relish the peace and solitude of this nest, even knowing that everything— oh yes, *everything*—is delicate and impermanent.

Once a vagabondess, always a vagabondess. I have not become someone different; rather, I have changed the container. I may pick up my lifestyle of constant movement in the near or distant future; even now, technically rooted in one place, I am constantly hitting the road for retreats, events, and visits to friends and family. Even when I have a whole month in San Jose, I am in constant flow with dance, yoga, and other kinetic explorations. Once a vagabondess, always a vagabondess. Maybe you already understand what I mean. If not, you'll find out soon enough. You'll see that "vagabondess" is not a label, and it is not a lifestyle. "Vagabondess" is a way of being, seeing, loving, discovering, and surrendering. It is a commitment to living in integrity, to chasing life, *always*, and to meeting oneself in every moment determined to fly higher, dive deeper, and grow bigger.

One does not simply stop being a vagabondess. It has nothing to do with how often you travel or where you live. It has everything to do with *how* you live in the small moments, every day. Because those moments add up to become your (impermanent, delicate) legacy. While my "container" looks a bit different than it did a couple years ago, I continue to live by the same principles:

- Feel the fear. Do it anyway.
- Trust, jump, and fly.
- Go and see.
- Hold lightly.
- Release expectations.
- Forget about "right" answers.

I have wondered at moments in this writing process if I could have simply written the above list and called it a day. One page is about the extent of the Internet's attention span, anyway. Everything I have shared in these pages—if I boil it down, and keep boiling, and keep boiling until I get at the pith—comes back to these few words. These are the themes that have lit up my journey from the beginning, becoming sharper and more pronounced all the time.

Feel the fear, and do it anyway. It's not about being fearless; it's about facing down our monsters and riding our fears through the dark, until they no longer have any power over us.

Trust, jump, and fly. Trust the Universe, trust humanity, trust your own damn self. Jump into the unknown, the void, and you'll learn how to fly, no doubt about it.

Go and see. Don't take anyone's word for it; go and find out for yourself. Write your own story, and carve your own path. No one else can do it for you.

Hold lightly. People, plans, and material belongings have minds of their own, and sometimes they disappear into the ether like socks in a dryer. It hurts less to let go when you soften your grip.

Release expectations. The gods laugh when we make plans. Expectations, say the Buddhists, the vagabonds, and the mystics, are the root of much suffering. Surrender to what is, let go of what might be, and what will come will far exceed anything you could have expected in the first place.

Forget about "right" answers. There is no right answer. "Wherever you go, there you are." Whatever path you choose, at any moment, there is your path.

It really is that simple. Famous last words. Why say more, right? Everything you really need to embrace your inner vagabondess is contained in that list. But that's the thing about platitudes. They don't galvanize us into action. They make neat memes to share on Instagram. They're nice for inspirational T-shirts or a pep talk to a friend who's feeling down. They sound good, and we know that their meaning runs deep, and yet we don't *do* anything with them. Unless, correct me if I'm wrong, when was the last time you changed your life path because of a nice quote?

It is my hope that the stories, ideas, and information shared in this book will support you to *act*. To seize the path you dream of, to "Throw off the bowlines. Sail away from the safe harbor. Catch the trade winds in your sails." Words on the page will not make it so. To walk the path of the vagabondess, you must… walk. Place one foot in front of the other. There is no other way. At best, I hope you can now walk with a bit more certainty and confidence—with fewer of the questions that block your path and more of the questions that urge you forward. There are thousands of vagabondesses like me out there; we are proof that it is possible. All those voices telling you it can't be done? We offer a different story.

So, what story will you write? I can't tell you that. Where will you walk? Only you know. What does your inner vagabondess look like, sound like, feel like when you let her out to play? I think you should probably go find out.

It is an honor to share my journey with you. I offer these pages to you in the service of freedom, bliss, growth, and adventure. May your challenges be surmountable, may your feet be happy, may your searches be puzzling, and may your heart be free.

I'll see you out there.

Be happy. Be free. Vagabond!

~ Toby Israel, 21 November, 2019

A WALK IN THE WOODS

Angel: Look how many beautiful trails there are! So many possibilities!

Devil: But, which is the best route to get where we're going?

Angel: We're not going anywhere, come on! Remember, we're just walking for the joy of it.

Devil: Right… right. Any path will do, just—

Angel: Just what? Any path will do. That's all.

Devil: Just, better be careful to choose the right one.

Angel: What do you mean? There is no right way to get there if we're not going to any "there" in particular. That's the whole point.

Devil: But, what if there are waterfalls on *that* trail? We wouldn't want to miss out on any natural wonders, would we?

Angel: And maybe there are unicorns on *this* trail. We just don't know until we try, do we? We'll see what we see and miss what we miss, and our walk will be exactly perfect.

Devil: Might as well just stay here. Wouldn't want to risk heading off in the wrong direction.

Angel: Not an option. We're walking. Anywhere. Somewhere. Nowhere. Does. Not. Matter. But we can't stay here. Life is moving, and we have to move too. So get up, count to three, and choose.

Devil: But, but... what about unicorns? And waterfalls? What about monsters? There could be monsters! No way, not worth the risk.

Angel: One.

Devil: Nope. Not going anywhere.

Angel: Two. Remember: There's no right way, only the way you choose to walk.

Devil: Not sold. Monsters, remember.

Angel: Wherever you walk, that is where you're going. Three.

Devil: ...

Angel: I'll choose, then. That way.

—

Acknowledgements

To Mom and Dad, who gave me all the tools I could need to grow my own wings. To my ancestors, who wandered not for adventure, but for survival. To each individual and community who welcomed me home with open arms, wherever I happened to be. To the road itself, whose lessons never run dry.

To my first readers, who lovingly offered their insights during the early stages of the revision process, and to my final readers who helped me cross the i's and dot the t's: Bud Shriner, Lindsey Hunt, Kara Linn, Soumyajeet Chattaraj. To my fabulous editor and dear friend, Pavita Singh. To my wonderful colleague and friend, August Tarantino, who is the reason I decided to crowdfund this project.

To the incredible friends, family, and strangers (new friends) who made this book possible through their generous support: Alyssa Thomas, Andrew Lebowitz, Earl Atta-Fynn, Edee Simon-Israel and Mark Israel (Mom and Dad), Jesse Begelfer, Halley McClure, Sharon Cragg, Skye Steritz, Steve Bonham (my first supporters on Patreon!). Adrián S. Mattei, Alena Shish, Alex Karzag, Alison Cohen, Alison Liedkie, Alyssa Thomas, Amalia Reisman, Amanda Christmann, Ana Maria Salaya, Anna Gnida, Anna Szczurek, Ann Levin, Antoine Brechu, Armin Diemer, August Tarantino, Ayumuitoe, Beth Weintraub Liberman, Betsy Blechman, Bette Ann Libby, Bianka Urbanovská, Bobbi Rood, Brandi Jacobs, Bria Weyker, Bryan Arturo, Caroline Caruso, Catt Panszczyk,

Cheryl Kiser, Clara Ramin, Constance Tarantino, Daniel Acosta González, Davide Quadrio, Deborah Atta-Fynn, Debra Hruschka, Diane DiCecco, Diego Bodart, Donna De Sani, Drew Dagenais, Durga Martin, Earl Atta-Fynn, Edee Simon-Israel and Mark Israel (Mom and Dad), Elise, Elizabeth Capotosto, Elle Ballinger, Ellen A Onderko, Emily Hodel, Erin Burdette, Erin K Lamb, Fernando Bolaños, Fiona Bechtler-Levin, Frank G Higginbotham, Gaby Prendas, Gilbert Zenner, Greg Pretnar, Halley McClure, Jacinta Astles, James Barford, Jean Pullen, Jesse Begelfer, Jill Cameron, Jill Forbes, Joao Lopes, Judith Foti, Judith Wolff, Julia Kratzer, Julie Hammonds, Keith Agoada, Kerry Thon, Kevin Sienkiewicz, Kim Wenger Hall, Kristin Ewton, Laura Lea Davidson, Lauren Garrett, Leslie Drew, Leslie Keehn, Lily Moon, Linda Wood, Lisa Zhu, Lynn Golan, Maddie Gilbert, Mandy Kimm, Marcie Maxfield, Marc Maksim, Maria Flores, Marina Garcia, Marisa Marzocchi, Mary Mastro, Matthew Mason, Max Cooper & Lindsey Hall, McKayla Baker, Melania Rojas, Melissa Rayburn, Michael Carbin, Michael Lim, Michelle Labow, Milena Trifunovic, Mitchell Gordon, Moksha Manifiesta, Mollie McGuire, Nancy Israel and Lonnie Powers (Aunt Nancy and Uncle Lonnie), Natalia Tertusio, Neni Lampropoulou, Paola Cabrera, Patrice Kaufman, Pavita Singh, Priya Tandon, Rae Maddox, Raffaello Manacorda, Robin Polishook, Rosanna Hertz, Sarah Foster, Sarah Kimsey, Sarah Wright, Sara Johnstone, Sara Tauben, Scott Israel (Brother Bear), Simone Youkel, Skye Steritz, Sofia Corrales, Stephanie Fields, Susan Israel (Aunt Susie), Sybil Collas, Tarn

Martin, Tawana Williams, The Yoga Barn in Stowe—Lisa Hagerty, Yaffa Quan-Weinreich.

And to the wild, wandering, wise sisters who have loved and supported me every step of my journey, and whose brilliant souls inspired this book.

Thank you. This book exists because of you!

Printed in Great Britain
by Amazon